Stock Market Investing for Beginners

Your Complete Step-by-Step Guide to Investing Intelligently in Stocks to Become Wealthy

Alex M. Peter

©2017

©Copyright 2017 by Alex M. Peter – All rights reserved.

This document is geared towards providing exact and reliable information in regards to the topic and issue covered. The publication is sold with the idea that the publisher is not required to render accounting, officially permitted, or otherwise, qualified services. If advice is necessary, legal or professional, a practiced individual in the profession should be ordered.

- From a Declaration of Principles which was accepted and approved equally by a Committee of the American Bar Association and a Committee of Publishers and Associations.

In no way is it legal to reproduce, duplicate, or transmit any part of this document in either electronic means or in printed format. Recording of this publication is strictly prohibited and any storage of this document is not allowed unless with written permission from the publisher. All rights reserved.

The information provided herein is stated to be truthful and consistent, in that any liability, in terms of inattention or otherwise, by any usage or abuse of any policies, processes, or directions contained within is the solitary and utter responsibility of the recipient reader. Under no circumstances will any legal responsibility or blame be held against the publisher for any reparation, damages, or monetary loss due to the information herein, either directly or indirectly.

Respective authors own all copyrights not held by the publisher.
The information herein is offered for informational purposes solely, and is universal as so. The presentation of the information is without contract or any type of guarantee assurance.

The trademarks that are used are without any consent, and the publication of the trademark is without permission or backing by the trademark owner. All trademarks and brands within this book are for clarifying purposes only and are the owned by the owners themselves, not affiliated with this document.

Introduction

This book – *Stock Market Investing for Beginners* aims to provide valuable information and guidance for anyone who wishes to try stock market investing for the first time. This is not intended for intermediate or advanced investor, although it may provide additional or use it as a refresher.

The stock market has a certain appeal that never fails to entice anyone. However, not everyone would dare try their hands on stock market investing due to its equally intimidating aura. The truth is, it is not that difficult to understand the ins and outs of stock market although the actual engagement may be a bit tricky.

This book aims to provide the right information regarding the stock market and you may feel less and less intimated about the subject as you learn more about it. You know that different individuals may not have the same level of knowledge and speed to grasp everything including stocks. However, this book will serve its purpose well by helping you understand all that you need to know about stock market investing. You may or may not learn as quickly as you plan, but you will surely grasp the essence of stock market investing.

It is my sincere hope that this book will guide you into your journey into the world of stock market investing.

Thanks again for buying this book and I hope you will learn a thing or two about investing in the stock market!

Table of Contents

Chapter 1: A Brief History of the Stock Market 5
Chapter 2: The Basics of Stock Market Investing 10
Chapter 3: What Are Stock Market Exchanges? 32
Chapter 4: Stock Market Lingo to Know 42
Chapter 5: Why Should You Invest in Stocks? 48
Chapter 6: Before You Begin - Find Out the Type of Investor You Are 53
Chapter 7: Open a Brokerage Account Now 63
Chapter 8: How to Properly Research A Company's Stock Prior to Investing 68
Chapter 9: How to Analyze Your Stock Before You Buy It 73
Chapter 10: The Top 15 Metrics You Must Examine Before Buying Any Stock 80
Chapter 11: Determine Your Basic Investment Philosophy and Goals 85
Chapter 12: How to Use Dividend and Dividend Reinvestment Plan to Compound Your Stock Investing Even More 90
Chapter 13: How to Buy Your First Stock to Start Your Stock Market Investment Journey 95
Chapter 14: How to Build a Portfolio of Stocks to Invest in 98
Chapter 15: Be Aware of the Costs to Investing in Stocks 102
Chapter 16: When to Sell a Stock 105
Chapter 17: How to Monitor and Grow Your Stocks 107
Chapter 18: Recommendations for Further Learning in Investing in Stocks 109
Conclusion 111

Chapter 1: A Brief History of the Stock Market

The modern world offers a lot of things that can make life more convenient and comfortable for everyone. However, an individual must pay a higher price to obtain such convenience. An ordinary worker needs to find other means to augment his finances just to make sure that they and their family would be able to live in comfort. Many would like to try stock market investing because they find it enticing. Unfortunately, most people who would like to try their hands on stock market investing also find it intimidating or foreign.

It is too early to say that you may not be able to be a good trader if you still haven't tried to get to know more about the ins and outs of stock market trading. In order to get to know it properly, it is best to learn something about its origin and basics first.

What Stock Market Is?

A stock market is not the same as the usual market that you know. It is a network of various economic transactions where sellers and buyers deal with stocks. Think of it also a share market because the stockholder actually owns a part of the company/business or gets a share of the company's assets (also known as stocks) and liabilities. However, the entire system it is not as simple as that.

Most investors refer to stock market as a collection of markets and exchanges. It involves issuing and trading of bonds, equities, and other forms of securities. When we say equity, it refers to ownership and not the money itself. For example, if you own two shares or stocks of Company B and your friend also owns the same number of stocks in the same company, you get the same number of votes when a company needs to make an important decision. Such occurrence usually happens during the company's annual meeting.

A company may have hundreds of shareholders and the percentage of each share depends on the number or amount of stocks that a particular shareholder owns. You need to understand that when you buy a stock or share, it does not mean that you own the entire company. Each stock represents only a minute fraction of the company. Your earnings (that dividend-paying companies give) will also depend on the amount of stocks that you own.

Like most businesses, the company that you have chosen to buy stocks from may experience some ups and downs. The value of your stocks depend on the current standing or status of the company that you partly own.

What Stock Market is Not

Some people believe that stock market investing can be classified as gambling. To be blunt, it should not be considered as gambling although there are risks involved – so does most things in life.

Let us assume that there is a certain game where you need to place a bet on any of the six cards on the table. You have decided to bet $50 on number six. If you win, you will get double the amount of your bet. If you lose, you will see your fifty-dollar disappear right before your eyes.

In stock market investing you will either gain or lose a certain amount of money, but you will not lose everything (unless something really bad happens to the company – I will show you how to prevent this from happening to you in this book). This goes to show that it is far from gambling, although there are also risks involved.

My aim in this book is to help you arrive at the right decision and guide you in choosing your investment wisely so you get more for your money. You will learn them all in the following chapters and I will try to guide you through each step of the way. First, let us take a look at stock market's early beginnings.

A Blast from the Past

In the twelfth century, there was a group in France known as **courtiers de change** that managed and regulated the agricultural communities' debts on the banks' behalf. The group traded with debts, and they could be regarded as the earliest brokers.

During the thirteenth century Bruges, Van der Beurze was a gentleman who owned a house that people believed to be a place where traders of commodities held regular meetings. In 1409, the said party of traders was later called **'Brugse Beurse'**.

Although the meetings were recognized before as something informal, the truth was that the meetings set in Antwerp were held inside a building. The owner of the said building was the same gentlemen who owned the house in Bruges. At that time, Antwerp became the favorite trading venue of most merchants. The idea very quickly reached Flanders as well as the neighboring countries. Soon, the cities of Ghent and Rotterdam also opened their own 'Beurzen' trading houses.

In mid-thirteenth century, the Venice bankers also became interested in government securities and began to trade them. However, in 1351 the government of Venice declared that it was forbidden to spread stories or rumors that have malicious intent to lower the price of government securities. During the fourteenth century in Verona, Genoa, Pisa, and Florence, the practice of trading government securities was once again initiated by the banks.

The governing bodies of the said city states allowed such trading to occur during that time because the mentioned places were independent territories that were not under a duke's jurisdiction. These states were governed by a citizen council that was duly elected. Italy's Organizations and businesses were the first to sell company stocks. In the United Kingdom, businesses were only able to sell company shares to investors in the mid or latter part of sixteenth century. From then on, many other countries began practicing the same type of trading.

In 1602, the Dutch East India country was established. It was the first joint-stock company wherein a stock holder may acquire a portion of the company or business, and he/she can buy more than one share. A shareholder is issued an ownership certificate wherein the portion of share that the shareholder purchased was clearly stated. The certificate also served as concrete proof of ownership. The said company was also the first trading company with fixed capital stock.

In the Amsterdam Stock Exchange, the company stocks were traded continually. Soon, others also followed. At that time, there were securities that had no current owners and there were people who took advantage of the situation and sold the said securities. The practice was known as **short selling**. Such practice was then classified as something illegal. The authorities banned it completely in 1610.

In the modern era, you can find stock markets around the world. Almost all countries have their own stock markets. The most famous stock markets and the biggest in the world are in USA, United Kingdom, France, Canada, Netherlands, China, India, Germany, South Korea, and Japan.

The First Stock Exchange

In 1801, the London Stock Exchange was officially established despite the fact that share issuance at that time was banned. It was a limited exchange that hindered the London Stock Exchange from hogging the limelight and dominating the market.

The emergence of the New York Stock Exchange or NYSE in 1817 marked a monumental moment in history. On its first day, the New York Stock Exchange did not waste any time and began trading stocks right away. Many believed that NYSE is the first stock exchange in the United States of America. The truth is, the Philadelphia Stock Exchange holds the title of being the first stock exchange in America. However, no one can deny that NYSE holds the title for being the most powerful stock exchange in the USA.

The London Stock Exchange became Europe's primary stock exchange, while the New York Stock Exchange became the primary exchange for America and the rest of the world.

Now that you get to know a bit about the stock market's past, it is time to proceed to the meatier topics.

Chapter 2: The Basics of Stock Market Investing

After getting to know a bit about the stock market's past, it is time to learn the basics of stock market investing. It is best to read thoroughly and digest everything that you learned. If something is vague, you need to go over it again to make things clear. There are times when you won't be able to process everything in one passing if this area is completely new to you so don't get too frustrated. Keep on reading for now.

What is a Stock?

It was already mentioned that when you buy stocks of a certain company or corporation, you become that company's part-owner and the same goes with everyone who bought stocks of that particular company. Thus, a stock is a share that shareholders or stock holders buy to become part owners of the company.

Does it also mean that you have the right to explore or access the areas within the company that are supposed to be off limits to unauthorized persons? Can you just grab anything that the company owns, like a table or printer, just because you also own a part of it? Do you have the right to hire or fire workers?

Many investment experts claimed that a stock embodies a shareholder's claim on the company's earnings and assets. They further added that when you buy more stocks of that company, the percentage of your ownership also increases. Regrettably, the definition of stock that many investment experts believed to be accurate has some flaws and therefore not entirely correct.

Just remember that you only own a small portion of the company and such ownership does not give you any authority to do things as you please with the company. Even if you own a significant amount of shares, you only have the right to vote when there's a major decision that concerns all shareholders of that company.

Digging Deeper

To be blunt, stock holders may be part owners of the company but they do not own the company or corporation. What the stock holders own are shares that the corporation issues. The law treats the corporations as legal persons. The corporations file taxes, can own properties, can borrow, can go to court, and other things. The notion that a corporation is a legal person (under the law) also means that the corporation is the rightful owner of its assets. This also explains why a shareholder cannot just take anything from the company or corporation, like a table or printer, because those are assets that the corporation owns. Those assets do not belong to the shareholders.

It is important to know the distinction between the properties that the corporation owns and the properties that the shareholders purchased. In case the corporation declares bankruptcy, it may need to get all its assets sold – take note that only the corporate assets must be sold. The shareholder's personal assets are not included. If you are a shareholder of the company that went bankrupt, the court has no right to force you to sell your shares. However, expect the value of your shares to fall drastically due to the company's bankruptcy. Likewise, when you declare bankruptcy, you also cannot sell the assets of the corporation to pay off the money that you owe your lender.

If you own a company share of 25%, it doesn't mean that you own one-fourth of that company. You cannot simply do anything you wish to do with the corporation or the assets that the corporation solely owns.

If you can't do anything with the corporation or touch its assets, what good does buying some shares bring? If you own a stock, you can express your opinion during a stock holder's meeting by exercising your right to vote. You can also take your share of company's profits in form of dividends when the company distributed them among shareholders. You also have the option to sell your stocks when you think that it is time to do so or when there's a need for you to do so.

You can indirectly maneuver the path that the corporation takes if you own the majority of shares. Your vote becomes extremely significant when choosing or appointing the board of directors. Why is it important to carefully choose the board of directors?

The primary function of the board of directors is to increase the value of the corporation. Hiring professional officers or managers, such as CEO or Chief Executive Officer, rests in the hands of the board of directors. For this reason, you need to make sure that the board has the intelligence and capabilities to make sound judgment.

In business, a company buying another company is a common thing. This is especially true if the company being bought can no longer sustain the costs of operation or other reason that compels the owner to sell his business. When the acquiring company has decided to buy another company, it actually buys all the shares and not the assets. There are times when the assets are also offered, including the employees. The acquiring company may retain all or some of the employees, and it may also decide to replace all the employees.

What about Ordinary Shareholders?

The ordinary shareholders also have the right to vote during the stockholder's meeting when there's a need to do so. If you are an ordinary shareholder, you are still entitled to receive dividends. The amount of dividends that each shareholder will receive depends on the number or percentage of shares that a particular stock holder owns. The more shares you own, the higher your dividend. Also, the amount of dividends that the company releases may also vary according to the profits that the company received during a certain period of operation.

Take note that there are many companies that don't give dividends. They usually reinvest the acquired profits to make the company flourish further. The retained earnings are still recorded in the value of stock. When you want to sell your shares, it is easy to find buyers when the stock is known to be profitable. You also need to determine the best time to trade your stocks.

Companies Raising Money

Companies that need to raise money can borrow from banks or issue bonds. You should know that bonds are different from stocks. Shareholders are practically part-owners (through stocks) of the company, while bondholders are the creditors (not banks) to the company. The bondholders are entitled to impose interest and to receive repayment of principal, which the shareholders don't enjoy.

In the event of company bankruptcy, the creditors (banks and/or bondholders) must be paid first before anyone else as stated under the law. The company is compelled to sell its assets in order to compensate the creditors. The shareholders have the least priority and often get nothing.

It may seem that buying stocks may not be a good investment at all. But you should think more deeply before you judge – why must you think that the company will go bankrupt? Keep in mind that it's just the worst case scenario that may not even come true, especially if the corporation where you own a stock is a stable big company.

Also, bondholders are only entitled to get the return based on the interest rate stated in the bond agreement. The shareholders may enjoy infinite returns that the profits provide. Historical record shows that stocks usually return eight to ten percent annually, while bonds have five to seven percent.

Stocks are usually issued by the companies to raise their capital to expand their operation or take on a new project. You can buy stocks from primary market (directly issued by the company) or secondary market (the seller is a shareholder).

The Most Typical Forms of Stocks

When a company is established, the only shareholders are the early investors (probably friends and family) and the co-founders. For example, if the company has two investors and two co-founders, each individual may own one-fourth of the total shares. As the company flourishes, it may need additional fund or capital to expand. The company may choose to issue shares or stocks to interested investors.

The originators may have lower percentage of shares compared to when they first started. During such stage, the company shares were considered private. In most cases, it is not easy to exchange private shares and there are only few shareholders who have them.

As the company continues to grow, there are times when the early investors may want to sell their shares. At the same time, the company may also need to gain more investments than the private investors can provide. The company, at this point, should make an initial public offering or IPO. Such move will transform it from private to public.

Companies may also issue these other two usual types of stock: common stock and preferred shares.

Common Stock

When you hear people discuss stocks, they are usually discussing the common stock. Most companies issue common stocks. In fact, a great majority of stocks are issued in such form.

When you buy a common stock, you can claim profits in form of dividends (a quarterly or a monthly payment to the shareholder of the stock) and you also have the right to vote. You are entitled to one vote per share to elect the board members.

Over time, common stock may yield higher returns compared to corporate bonds. However, it is riskier to invest in common stock because the shareholder may lose large portion of the investment when the company happens to go out of business. The common stock holders get the least priority when the company goes bankrupt, and that means they need to wait until the creditors and preferred stock holders get paid. Usually, there's only little amount of funds (or none at all) left to be shared among common stock holders.

Preferred Stock

Preferred stocks are similar to bonds. Preferred stock holders have no voting rights, although there are companies that may offer the same privileges that common stock holders enjoy.

Preferred stock investors usually get a fixed dividend. Common stock investors get variable dividends (sometimes high, low, or nothing at all) as declared by the board of directors. The company may also choose to re-purchase the preferred stock shares from the stock holders at any time. Preferred stock shareholders are usually offered a premium price.

In the event of liquidation, preferred stock shareholders are next in line after the creditors have been paid off. You can think of preferred stocks as something between common shares and bonds.

Common stocks and preferred shares are the typical forms of stocks issued by most companies. It is also possible for companies to create a different form or type of stock to meet the requirements of their investors.

The most typical reason of most companies in creating share classes is to congregate the voting power within a particular group. The different classes of shares have different voting privileges.

Stock Market and Trading

This section will help you understand the basics regarding how stock market works and why stocks have such response. You will also learn the things that an investor should know and help you make the right choices.

The stock market has millions of investors that may have opposing views. One investor may want to sell a particular security and another investor may want to buy it. Under certain circumstances, one investor may actually be losing money, while the other one may gain more than what he expects from the transaction.

You cannot explicitly say that the seller is the one who profits from the transaction and the buyer loses his money. Keep in mind that the value of stocks may fluctuate within the day.

The seller may actually be the one who will lose some profits from the transaction. It is possible for the price of stock that he wants to sells to go up in the next couple of hours. What if a clever buyer suddenly grabbed the opportunity and immediately buys it from him? The seller will no longer able to enjoy the profit that his stock should have given him simply because it's no longer in his possession. The buyer, on the other hand, gets to reap all the profits in the end.

If you want to be a wise investor, you need to know more about the investment that perked your interest and study the market's response to it. You should consider all the aspects of your target stock before you begin trading.

The Fluctuating Stock Prices

There are many things that affect the rise and fall of stock prices. The usual culprits are social and political unrest, natural disasters, supply and demand, and the absence or large quantity of suitable alternatives. There are times when media and the opinions of famous investors regarding certain companies or stocks can also affect the market.

These factors together with the relevant information that have already been disseminated may create a particular type of sentiment as well as corresponding number of sellers and buyers. If the number of sellers greatly exceeds the number of buyers, stock prices have tendency to go down. When there are more buyers than sellers, the price will surely go up.

Why is it Difficult to Predict?

Let us take a look at a scenario where stock prices have been rising for several years as an example. Investors know that sooner or later a correction will surely occur that will bring the stock prices down. The day when the selloff will happen and what will trigger are only some of the things that we are uncertain and may even find it difficult to understand. There are investors who will patiently wait on the sidelines with their money on hand and wait for the auspicious time before they dive in.

Those who are more than willing to take the risk may not hesitate to dive in because they already expect that the cash return is low, and they find it unbearable to earn nothing while seeing the stocks get higher. This leads to a couple of questions. If you are the one on the sidelines, what signs do you need to watch out for that will alert you when to get in? If you are already in, what are the signs that you need to see that tell you that it is time get out? If it is easy to predict the stock market trend, then these questions should have never popped up.

There are actually three issues that a prudent investor should think about. The first issue is to understand the point in time when the stock prices have fair value. The second issue is to analyze the event that could cause possible downturn. The third issue involves learning the decision-making process of individuals. Take a look at the following in order to see the big picture:

Stock Valuation

The market activity determines the actual price of a stock. A prudent investor often makes a comparison between the actual price of a stock and its fair value. Take a look at this example:

If a stock is being offered at $40 per share and its fair value is $45, you may actually gain a worthy purchase when you have decided to buy the stock. If it is being offered at $40 and its fair value is only $35, the stock could be considered overvalued. It is wise to avoid purchasing such stock.

What is the fair value of a stock and how do you compute it? Ideally, the computation is done using some standardized formula. But, there are many ways to come up with the given figure. You can:

1. Combine the value of all the assets of the company and include it on the balance sheet, and subtract the liabilities and depreciation.

2. Determine the intrinsic value of the stock. You can compute the intrinsic value by determining the net current value of the future earnings of the company.

We just briefly discussed the two methods, and there are still other methods out there for you to try. There are times when the methods may yield slightly different results. When that happens, it is quite difficult to know if the price of a certain stock is overvalued, undervalued, or fairly valued. Even if the stock is overvalued, that doesn't necessarily mean that the price will fall when the investors suddenly sell. The truth is that the price of a stock may remain overvalued for quite a while. This is also the reason why it may become troublesome to decide whether to buy or sell when the price of stock is dependent on the sentiment of the market.

Triggering Event

It is advisable to know the events that may possibly cause a trend reversal. A wise investor will always try to know or find out the things that are happening around him and the world, which may have an impact on his investments. You must be able to analyze things in order to arrive at a sound decision.

The Human Decision Process

This is the most interesting among the three issues. Each person has emotional and logical components. You may use your logical component to analyze a certain situation and event to help you come up with a sound decision. But when the time to finally make your decision, you may suddenly refer to your emotions to help you decide.

When buying a car, for example, the first thing that you might do is conduct a proper research about the different car engines to find out the best one that suits your preference. You may also want to consider the fuel efficiency of the car that you intend to purchase. You also need to know the amenities and other items that come with your car purchase. However, when it's time to decide, there may still be other things that might pop in your mind. You might wonder how you may appear in public's eyes when you are in the driver's seat. Does the car match your image well?

When making decisions regarding your investments, whether to buy or sell stocks, bear in mind that there will always be an investor who is interested on the things that you want to put up for sale. There are also investors who are selling the stock that you have wanted to purchase for so long. It is best if you can process the relevant data immediately and arrive at a good decision. But, you also need to understand that it's impossible to know all the things that you need to know and process everything without being biased. You might even end up making a sub-par decision. Such dilemma also occurs with individuals that are already considered the most analytical.

When is the Best Time to Buy and Sell?

There are two most important decisions that you need to make as an investor, and they are: when to **buy** and when to **sell your stocks**. You buy stocks with fair market value and only sell them at the opportune time where your investment can give you the most profits or if you sell at the wrong time, you could lose some of your gains or all of them.

You must grab the opportunity to buy stocks when other investors are being pessimistic. If other investors are actively being optimistic, it is the best time to sell your acquired stocks.

When you plan to buy stocks, bear in mind that you will be able to gain a greater chance of getting a high return if you purchase the stock right after its price has fallen. It is foolish to buy stocks right after their prices have risen. However, you still need to be cautious at all times. You need to be aware of other factors that may trigger the sudden rise or fall of stock prices.

Let us use Company B for our example. Let us assume that the stocks of Company B have declined by 20%, 30%, or more. The first question you need to ask yourself is why did the stocks of the company suddenly fall? You need to investigate whether the other stocks within the same industry has experienced the same thing. If the other companies also suffered such loss, you need to find out the severity of the decline and make a comparison. You may also need to find out whether the entire stock market has crashed.

If a wide array of market or other stocks within the same industry have performed quite well and only Company B experienced such decline, there may be a problem within Company B that triggered the sudden decline. It would be wise for you to follow the buy/sell discipline and stick to it.

Important Reminders

As an investor, there are certain things that you need to keep in mind when dealing with stocks.

1. The stock market is rather complicated for a novice investor, but you will be able to grasp everything that you need to know within a certain time. Not every individual share the same level of understanding or aptitude.

2. It is best to avoid listening to the "hot tip" that a colleague may have about stocks when he begins discussing it in the lunchroom.

3. There are different reasons that affect the rise and fall of stock prices. Some can be too complex to understand, especially by a novice like you.

4. When you invest, zero is the only sure bottom. You may want to include adding protection (i.e., options, stop orders, and others).

5. Always make sure that the stocks that you buy are truly worth your money.

6. Unless you are someone with penchant for taking risk, you may want to avoid putting all your money in one particular stock.

It usually takes years before you become well adept in dealing with financial markets and handling stocks. You may want to consider seeking help from a financial expert that you can trust and take you under his/her wings to guide you properly. Venturing into the unknown territory alone may cost you more than you expect.

The Different Trading Orders

You also need to determine the type of trade that you would like to have. There are also different trading orders that you need to know.

Market Order

This order tells the broker to buy or sell stocks at the best price available. For example, the stock quote gives the following data:

Bid: $129.75 (100)

Offer: $130 (50)

Last: $129.90 (200)

The quote informs us that the last trade was 200 shares at $129.90 and 50 shares are offered at $130. What if you have a market order to purchase 75 shares? Let us assume that 100 additional shares are offered at $130.10. Your broker would purchase 50 shares at $130 and 25 shares at $130.10 (being the next best price).

A market order can only guarantee that you will be able to get the number of shares that you need and it does not guarantee the price. However, the broker will try to purchase the stocks at the best price. The order is said to be 'filled' when the order has been completed.

A market order is most suitable for buyers or sellers who are more concerned in filling the size of the order rather than the price.

Limit Order

The market order focuses on the size of the order, while the limit order is concerned with the price that you are willing to trade. Let us use the same stock quote in the given example above. This time, you want to buy 75 shares at $130 and the cost should not exceed your ceiling price.

The 50 shares offered at $130 will be bought immediately, while you wait for some seller to bring down their price to meet your demand. With limit order, completing the size of the order is not the priority.

A limit order can also come as all-or-none or AON, which simply means that you only buy shares when your price and size of order are both satisfied. Let us say that you have an AON and you want to buy 100 shares at $130. You are not going to buy the 50 shares being offered unless another 50 shares at the same price come along.

A limit order is most suitable for buyers or sellers who are more concerned in getting the price they want rather than filling the size of the order.

Stop Order

If you have a stop order, the execution of your trade will only commence when the price of the security that you intend to purchase or sell has finally reached your **target price or stop price**. The moment your target stock has reached the said price, a stop order basically turns into a market order that must be filled.

Let us assume that you own stock RVA, which currently trades at $30, and you put a stop order to sell it at $25. The moment stock RVA drops below $25, your order will be filled. This also gives you an opportunity to limit your losses, and it is also called a **stop-loss order**.

You can also use stop order to guarantee your profits. Let us assume that you bought stock ASA at $20 per share and it is currently trading at $30 per share. If you put a stop order at $26, you will still have a guaranteed profit of $6 per share and you can enjoy bigger profits when the market order can be filled right away. Investors who are unable to properly monitor their stocks can benefit a lot from stop orders.

Stop order has one disadvantage – there's no guarantee that the order can be filled at your preferred price. Understand that once the stop order has been initiated, it automatically turns into a market order where the size of the order must be filled at the best price. It is possible that the best price at that time may be lower than your specified price.

You need to be careful about where to set a stop order. It may bring unfavorable outcome if it is initiated via a short-term fluctuation in the price of your stock.

Immediate-Or-Cancel (IOC) Order

Orders may come with instructions about its time frame or validity. An IOC order must be executed immediately or it gets cancelled. It is commonly used in conjunction with a limit order.

Other Orders

A fill-or-kill (FOK) order is a combination of IOC order and AON order. The IOC and AON orders must be used together. Otherwise you won't be able to initiate FOK.

There's also a day order, which is a stop or limit order that remains valid until the trading day ends. It will no longer be active the following day.

A GTC or good-til-cancelled order remains active until an instruction that cancels it is released. It may remain active for many days.

Margin Trading and Short Selling

Margin trading is being offered by many brokerages. Margin trading allows clients to borrow money in case they run out of funds to buy shares. A client can only borrow the additional amount of money that his/her account needs to purchase the share.

Margin is also allowed for short selling. A market participant may borrow someone's stock shares and sell them with an intention of buying back the borrowed shares at a lower price in the future. A short seller is actually betting that stock price will decline and not rise.

Basic Rules of the Stock Market that You Should Know

If you recognize the companies listed on the stock exchanges and you are somewhat familiar with some of them, you may find yourself in a disadvantaged position. Rather than gaining benefits, you may find yourself being tempted in buying the stocks of the company that is making your favorite products. It may also be due to your closeness with the people that work in the company or the company's main office happens to be in your hometown.

Always keep in mind that a prudent investor should always choose a strong company and must not be influenced by reasons stated above. It is well and good if the company that produces your favorite items is also a strong one.

So you won't go astray, remember these rules:

1. **You need to focus on the price of stock**

Different educated traders have different set of criteria when investing their money and it is impossible for two investors to have the same set of criteria. But, there's one thing that they will focus on and take into consideration – the price.

A wise trader can profit a lot even from poorly run company if the price of stock proved to bring more benefits and advantages to the trader. However, you must be able to sense proper timing – get in when the auspicious time arrives and get out when there's already enough profit. Don't look forward to gaining much profit from such companies.

2. Make sure that your stocks stay liquid

To be blunt, the stock must be actively traded (a daily volume of at least 100,000 shares). You need to make sure that you won't find yourself in a situation wherein you remain stuck where you are because the other side has no traders. You also need to stick to tickers that cost $50 and below. For tickers with price above $50, many traders find the requirements to maintain the liquidity distracting.

3. It is best to practice before you take the plunge.

Don't try the broad market until you are confident and sure that you can take on the big league. You should consider monitoring a few tickers and finding out their trading range. Remember the first reminder: focus on the price.

How to Read a Stock Table or Quote

As a stock trader, it is important that you know how to read the stock table or quote.

52W high	52W low	Stock	Ticker	Div	Yield %	P/E	Vol 00s	High	Low	Close	Net chg
$45.39	19.75	ResMed	RMD			52.5	3831	42.00	39.51	41.50	-1.90
11.63	3.55	Revlon A	REV				162	6.09	5.90	6.09	+0.12
77.25	55.13	RioTinto	RTP	2.30	3.2		168	72.75	71.84	72.74	+0.03
31.31	16.63	RitchieBr	RBA			20.9	15	24.49	24.29	24.49	-0.01
8.44	1.75	RiteAid	RAD				31028	4.50	4.20	4.31	+0.21
s38.63	18.81	RobtHalf	RHI			26.5	6517	27.15	26.50	26.50	+0.14
51.25	27.69	Rockwell	ROK	1.02	2.1	14.5	6412	47.99	47.00	47.54	+0.24
1	2	3	4	5	6	7	8	9	10	11	12

Above is sample stock table. It may look nothing but a collection of numbers, but the data that the table contains can help you a lot. The numbers 1 to 12 that you see below the table are the group numbers. You can see the explanation for each column or group in the succeeding paragraphs.

Group 1 contains the highest prices at which a stock is traded over the previous 52 weeks (one year). This typically does not include the previous day's trading.

Group 2 contains the lowest amounts of a traded stock for the past 52 weeks. The past day's trading is not included.

Group 3 contains the company name and stock type. It lists the name of the company. It is a common stock if you can't find special symbols or letters after the company name. There are different types of shares, and each type of share has its own symbol. The symbol "pf" at the end of the company name means preferred stock, which informs you that the company issues such type of stock.

Group 4 contains the ticker symbol, which usually use three letters to identify a certain share. When you watch TV programs that tackle marketing or about money, you must have noticed that figures constantly move on your TV screen. It is called the ticker tape, which contains the current stock prices along with the symbol.

You need to search for the company's ticker symbol when you go online to look for quotes.

Group 5 contains the amount of dividend for each share. The quote indicates the yearly dividend payment for each share. A blank space simply indicates that no dividends are currently being paid by the company.

Group 6 contains dividend yield, which is a dividend return in percentage form. This can be computed this way:

Yearly Dividends for each Share ÷ Share Price

Group 7 contains the ratio for price / earnings, it can be calculated using this formula:

Present Stock Price ÷ Per Share Earnings

Group 8 contains the trading volume, which indicates the day's total count of traded shares. You need to add "00" after the listed number to get the actual number of traded shares.

Group 9 contains the day high and group 10 contains the day low. Both groups show the traded stock price range the entire trading day. Group 9 indicates the maximum prices and group 10 indicates the lowest paid amounts for the stock.

Group 11 contains the last recorded trading price for that day at closing. It is customary to write the entire stock listing in bold letters when the price closing amount is more than or less than 5% of the previous day's closing price.

Take note, you can't be certain that you will get the same amount when you purchase the stock in the following day. Understand that the price is forever changing. Even if trading for the day in the local exchange has ended, there are still other stock exchanges all over the world that is still operating. The outcome of their trade may have an effect on the entire stock market that can also bring some changes in stock prices. In stock trading, the term "close" also serves as past performance indicator.

Group 12 contains net change, which is the worth change in dollars between the current stock price and the closing price from the previous day. When net change is positive, the stock is "up for the day".

You can always go back to the topic when you need to. Always keep in mind that it is best to go to the next discussion when everything is clear.

Chapter 3: What Are Stock Market Exchanges?

Stock market exchanges are organized, regulated financial markets, where securities (shares, bonds, and notes) are bought and sold at prices dictated by the law of supply and demand. Stock exchanges fundamentally serve as:

1. Primary markets where corporations, municipalities, governments, and other incorporated bodies are permitted to raise capital by offering productive ventures to investors.

2. Secondary markets where investors can meet to buy and sell securities from or to other investors, thus reducing possible risk and maintaining liquidity.

Stock exchanges compel the participants (all listed and trading parties) to follow their statutory requirements, stringent rules, and listing requirements.

In the older exchanges, trades are conducted on the 'trading floor' of the particular exchange. The traders use the open outcry system wherein they shout orders and instructions. In the modern exchanges, the trades are done in a more peaceful, well-behaved manner. The business is usually conducted online or over the phone.

All through the trading day, buyers enter competitive bids and sellers enter competitive orders. In some European exchanges, they utilize a method that uses round-robin calls. This method is called 'periodic auction'.

Understand that a stock market exchange does not own shares. Its main purpose is to serve as market or venue where stock buyers and sellers meet. There are different stock exchanges all over the world and the three largest are **the New York Stock Exchange** (NYSE), **London Stock Exchange** (LSE), and the **Tokyo Stock Exchange** (TSE).

Most beginners may most likely use a broker to trade stocks. It is also important for you to understand the relationship between the different companies or corporations and the stock exchanges. Know that the different exchanges have their own requirements that can help them provide protection to investors.

Function and Purpose of a Stock Exchange

The main function of a stock exchange is to provide smooth transactions associated with securities that must be bought or sold. Stock buyers and sellers alike can easily track any changes in price or volume of securities or stocks being traded in the stock exchange.

When companies or corporations need to add capital, they usually issue shares to investors, who are likely to sell them in the future and gain profits. Different stock holders have different reasons for buying and selling shares. Some of the reasons are to prepare for their retirement, secure their child's college education, buy a house, and others.

Whatever their reason may be, the stock holders are not likely to hold on to their shares. Somehow, they are certain that at some point in time they would be able to find a buyer for their shares in the secondary market, which is popularly known as stock exchange.

The presence of stock exchange makes it convenient and simple to buy and sell stock shares. Investors don't need to go to friends, community members, and other places just to buy their target stocks or sell their shares. Without stock exchange, the shareholders may experience some difficulties in finding buyers or sellers.

It is still possible to find sellers and buyers of stocks even without stock exchange, but it may take a long time to achieve what you want. Also, there's a lack of transparency. You may not be able to get the fair value for the stocks because you won't be able to get access to a stock quote, which the stock exchange provides.

Role of a Stock Exchange

The stock exchange has different roles and each one is highly important in helping the country achieve economic development. Stock exchanges can measure and control a country's growth.

The stock exchange is a place where stock trading transactions are executed. The transactions are usually done by your broker or you can trade directly if you hold a membership with that particular stock market.

Here are some of the important roles of stock exchanges:

1. Raise the capital of a corporation or company.

Exchanges make it easy, simple, and convenient for investing public and companies selling shares to meet and go about their business. Stock sellers and buyers only need to visit a stock exchange to achieve their purpose.

2. Help mobilize savings for investment.

The stock exchanges can help the public get more from their savings by presenting high yielding investments. The higher yield can be beneficial to both stock holders and the national economy.

3. Ensure equality in profit sharing.

Stock exchanges make sure that both casual and professional stock investors will be able to get their fair share of profit.

4. Facilitate the growth of a company.

The exchanges can help many companies attain the needed expansion and growth through fusion or acquisition.

5. Create investment prospects for small investors.

Small investors can buy small number of shares so they too can have a chance to participate in the large companies' growth.

6. Provide good corporate governance.

Companies must follow the stock exchanges' stringent rules if they truly want to get listed. Due to such rigidness, listed public companies have able to gain better record management as compared with privately held companies.

7. Aid the government in raising capital for projects related to the development of a region.

The exchanges can help government to raise fund for projects or activities that can help make the region prosper. An investor can take advantage of the bonds that the government issues. Buying a government bond means lending money to the government. The bonds are more secure, and sometimes there are also tax benefits that can be gathered from the said transaction.

8. Serve as economy's barometer.

The stock exchange has the capability to regulate the fluctuations in stock prices.

How do Companies Get Listed in the Stock Exchange

To get listed in the stock exchange, a company must first conduct an initial public offering or IPO. When conducting an IPO, a company sells shares to public shareholders or the primary market. The shareholders who would like to sell their shares and buyers who seek good stocks to buy usually go to the stock exchange.

The IPO Process

The entire process of turning a private company into a public one can be time consuming but still worth it. A company may need to hire an investment bank, which will take care of the initial public offering.

While it is true that individual investors from IPO are initially the ones to provide the company with additional capital, the investment bank is the one that usually finances the transaction. The investment bank provides the capital to the issuing company prior to going public with their stocks.

Here is the step by step IPO process:

1. The company that needs to get listed in the stock exchange must hire an underwriter or investment bank. The underwriter will help and guide the company through its IPO process.

2. The company is required to register with Securities and Exchange Commission (SEC) and notify the agency that the company would like to go public. It is best to have an attorney to avoid misinterpretation of statements or information.

3. The company must write a detailed record regarding its history, growth potential, services, products, and market share. A list regarding risk disclosures (must comply with the regulations of SEC) must be included. The company must also maintain factual and accurate information regarding their operations and financial status. The company must work with their attorney to make sure that they would be able to comply with SEC regulations.

4. The company must establish good relationship with the brokerage houses as well as investment bank, which can provide a lot of help in the success of the IPO process.

5. There is a need to promote the IPO with prospective shareholders at media outlets and brokerage houses all over the country. Such move can help create noise about the company's offer even before the IPO is approved by SEC.

6. Respond to SEC's queries without delay and obtain the approval of SEC. The company and its attorney must review all the documents before submission.

7. Determine the IPO price.

The company may decide to go public through a stock exchange, such as National Association of Securities Dealers

Automated Quotations (NASDAQ), New York Stock Exchange (NYSE), Toronto Stock Exchange, and others. The different stock exchanges may ask for additional requirements that the company must fulfill.

The Different Stock Exchanges

Here are some of the leading stock exchanges in the world:

1. **New York Stock Exchange** (NYSE)

NYSE is located in New York City, and was founded on May 17, 1792. The registered owner of NYSE is Intercontinental Exchange. It has listed market capitalization of $19.6 trillion in 2016. It occupies the top spot in the list of world's largest stock exchange.

When trading in NYSE, specialists usually grace the trading floors of the exchange with their presence. Every specialist handles a particular stock that they can deal with utmost confidence. These specialists won't allow the electronic-only exchanges threaten their existence. They continuously enhance their skills and try to be more competent.

The NYSE is still the most prestigious and largest exchange in the world. Companies that are listed on the NYSE are expected to possess great credibility, which can attract a lot of investors. Most investors know that these companies must first meet NYSE's initial listing requirements before they can get listed. They must also be able to comply with NYSE's annual maintenance requirements, such as the companies' price per share must be $4 and above and should have more than $40 million market capitalization.

2. National Association of Securities Dealers Automated Quotations (NASDAQ)

NASDAQ is located in New York City, and was founded on February 4, 1971. The registered owner of NASDAQ is NASDAQ, Inc. It has listed market capitalization of $7.8 trillion in 2016. It occupies the second spot in the list of world's largest stock exchange.

NASDAQ is an electronic exchange, and it also sometimes called "screen-based" because buying and selling can be accomplished using a computer and telecommunications network. Dealers must carry their own stock inventory. They prepare themselves to buy and sell NASDAQ stocks, and they also need to post their bid and ask prices.

The listing requirements of NASDAQ are similar to that of NYSE. Companies that would like to get listed on NASDAQ should maintain a minimum price of $4 per stock share. If a company fails to maintain the requirements of NASDAQ, it can be delisted.

3. **Toronto Stock Exchange** (TSX)

Toronto Stock Exchange (TSX) is located in Toronto, Ontario, Canada, and was officially founded on October 25, 1861. The registered owner of TSX is TMX Group. It has listed market capitalization of $2 trillion in 2016. It occupies the fourth spot in the 2016 list of growing stock value.

TSX is Canada's largest stock exchange. It was established in 1852, but the TSX's official foundation happened on 1861. The owner of TSX is TMX, which is owned by Maple Group Acquisition Corporation.

The TSX became the second (Montreal Exchange was the first at that time) official stock exchange in Canada in 1878 when the Act of the Ontario Legislature formally incorporated it.

Back then, only 18 securities were listed and daily trading must be limited only to half-hour sessions.

TSX was referred to as TSE until 2001, and still maintained the full name Toronto Stock Exchange. TSX is North America's third largest stock exchange in terms of capitalization. In 2009, it merged with Montreal Stock Exchange and the parent company became known as TMX Group. TSX trades are done electronically since they abolished their trading floor in 1997.

4. **London Stock Exchange** (LSE)

London Stock Exchange (LSE) is located in London, England. In 1571, it was known as the Royal Exchange and London Stock Exchange was officially founded in 1801. The registered owner of LSE is the London Stock Exchange Group. It has listed market capitalization of $3.5 trillion in 2016. It occupies the fifth spot in the 2016 list of world's largest stock exchange.

Although LSE has been around for hundreds of years, the London Stock Exchange Group that officially owned it was only established in 2007. Milan Stock Exchange and LSE merged in 2007. LSE once had a failed merger with TSX.

5. **Tokyo Stock Exchange** (TSE)

Tokyo Stock Exchange (TSE) is located in Tokyo, Japan, and was founded on May 15, 1878 and was known then as Tokyo Kabushiki Torihikijo. It changed its name to Tokyo Stock Exchange in May 16, 1949. Japan Exchange Group Inc. (Tokyo Stock Exchange Group, Inc.) is the registered owner of TSE. It has listed market capitalization of $5.1 trillion in 2016. It occupies the third spot in the 2016 list of world's largest stock exchange. It also occupies the top spot in the list of Asia's largest stock exchanges.

Don't confuse TSE (that stands for Tokyo Stock Exchange) with Toronto Stock Exchange (TSX).

The Nikkei 225 index achieved a record high of 38,957 in December, 1989. During such time, TSE has acquired 60% of market capitalization worldwide. However, its combined market capitalization significantly shrank over the next twenty years as the economy of Japan struggled with recession and Nikkei plunge.

6. **Shanghai Stock Exchange** (SSE)

Shanghai Stock Exchange (SSE) is located in Shanghai, China, and was founded on November 26, 1990. It has listed market capitalization of $4.1 trillion in 2016. It occupies the fourth spot in the 2016 list of world's largest stock exchange. It also occupies the second spot in the list of Asia's largest stock exchanges.

SSE is the world's largest stock exchange that is still controlled and owned by a government. It is mainland China's largest stock exchange that operates as a non-profit entity. The China Securities Regulatory Commission is the one responsible for SSE's operation. It is considered one of the most restrictive among the major stock exchanges when it comes to trading and listing standards.

You also need to learn some stock market terminologies to make things easier.

Chapter 4: Stock Market Lingo to Know

There are stock market terminologies that you should know. You don't need to learn them all – but just few important and commonly used terms that you may encounter every now and then. You will be able to learn all the stock market terms later on, especially when you have been trading for a long time.

Ask Price

It is the lowest price that the stock seller is determined to accept.

Bid Price

It is the highest price that the stock buyer is willing to pay for a certain volume of shares.

Blue Chip Stocks

These stocks are offered by well-known and leading companies that have been operating for many years. The companies that offer them are usually large and financially sound, and they have market capitalization in billions of dollars. These companies also religiously pay dividends to stock holders. As a beginner, these are the types of companies you want to start investing in not the small and often risky ones. As you become more familiar and comfortable in your investment style and decision, you can transition into investing into more riskier or smaller stocks.

Bull Market

It is a financial market when the prices of securities or stocks are expected to rise or already rising. The term "bull market" is commonly used to point out a particular stock market but it can also pertain to any entity that can be traded, such as commodities, bonds, and currencies.

Bear Market

It is a bull market's opposite – the prices of securities or stocks are expected to fall or already falling. The widespread pessimism causes the downward spiral of stock market. Many stock holders and buyers anticipate losses. At the same time, pessimism intensifies and the number of stocks being sold continues to increase. Fear is the predominant sentiment in the market and investors generally dump their stock in hopes of stopping their loss.

Broker

A broker is a regulated professional who is usually connected with a brokerage firm. The broker buys and sells securities or stocks on behalf of a client via a stock exchange or over a counter. The broker gets a commission or fee as compensation.

Close

The term 'close' can mean a lot of things in stock market. It can refer to a market close or end of trading session or day. It can also mean exiting a trade, the last price that's traded for the day, or financial transaction's final procedure.

Derivative

In stock market, the derivative is a contract between two or more individuals. The fluctuations in the underlying asset determine its value. The typical underlying assets include interest rates, currencies, commodities, market indexes, bonds, and stocks.

Day Trading

The term day trading is commonly used in stock market and foreign-exchange or forex, and it is when buying and selling of a security happens within one trading day.

Dividend

A dividend is a portion of company's earnings or profits that must be distributed to its shareholders who bought stocks that earn dividend. The board of directors decides for the amount of dividend that must be given to shareholders. The amount that each stock holder should receive depends on their class and number of shares. Dividends can be shares of stock, cash, or other property.

Equity

In stock market, equity can be a stock or other security that represents ownership interest. Generally, equity is assets minus liabilities. However, ownership of stocks in public company does not normally come with corresponding liabilities.

Initial Public Offering (IPO)

When a private company offers its stock to the public for the first time, it is known as IPO. It is usually offered by younger, smaller companies that need to acquire additional capital to expand. However, large privately owned companies can also do the same when they choose to join other publicly traded businesses.

Order

This can be a buy or sell order – depending on the needs of a trader. It must be executed or filled immediately in accordance with the instructions that come with the order. (The different orders were already discussed in the previous chapter.)

Market Capitalization

It is the outstanding stocks' market value of a company or corporation. To get the market capitalization of a certain company, you need to multiply the share price of the stock by the number of shares outstanding.

Moving average

It is a tool for simple technical analysis that helps smooth out price data by continually providing an updated average price. The average price is the result of monitoring the price within a specific period of time that the trader chooses. It could be 15 minutes, 10 days, 25 weeks, or other time period.

Margin Call

It occurs when there's a need for the investor to increase his/her purchasing power to acquire more stocks without the need to make an outright payment from his/her pocket. You can treat it as an SOS call for help when the investor is running low on funds to purchase the stock and he/she needs to buy it right away. The investor must have a margin account.

Market Order

A market order is the simplest form of order where it demands the volume of ordered stocks to get filled immediately by buying the stocks at the best available price. It does not give a price ceiling because the priority is to fill up the volume stated in the order. However, the broker is still expected to purchase the stock at the best price.

Short Sale

A short sale is selling a stock or security that the seller does not own. It could be a borrowed stock that the seller has to sell so he/she can buy it back at a lower price later.

Stop Order

It is a type of order that aims to limit losses on the part of the investor. It requires the broker to sell a stock or security when a certain price has been reached.

Portfolio

It is a consortium of financial assets such as bonds, stocks, and cash equivalents. It also includes their funds counterparts – close, mutual, and exchange-traded funds. A portfolio can be managed by professionals in the financial world, held directly by investors, or both (at the same time).

Quote

A quote is a last price that a buyer and seller have agreed to close the transaction or trade the stock or security. It can also be the most current prices and numbers of shares that can be traded.

Rally

It is a period of sustained price increases in bonds, stocks, or indexes. Such price movement usually happens during a bull or a bear market.

Sector

It is a group of stocks that create profits or revenue from similar area of business.

Stock Symbol

A stock symbol or ticker symbol is an abbreviated term that is unique to each publicly traded stock on a particular stock market. It serves as an ID of a particular stock.

Trading Session

It is a period of time in a financial market that starts when the opening bell resonates and ends with the closing bell. All orders for the day must be placed after the opening bell sounds and before the closing bell reverberates.

Volume

It is the number of contracts or shares traded within a given period of time.

Yield

The income return on an investment, such as dividend or interest, is known as yield. It is usually expressed as yearly percentage rate.

Chapter 5: Why Should You Invest in Stocks?

Why are there people who are interested to invest in stocks? Is it truly beneficial and advantageous to buy stocks for investment? To be frank, investing in stock market can bring lots of benefits and advantages. However, the problem is that you need to be careful in your judgment and should be able to weigh things to make the right decision.

Here are some of the good things that stock investing can bring:

Passive Income

In a nutshell, passive income is something that generates money on a regular basis without the need to oversee it regularly. You don't even need to exert too much effort to create and maintain it. However, it is still advisable to conduct minimum monitoring to make sure that nothing is amiss.

You can make an upfront investment in terms of time and/or money just to start things up. Once the ball gets rolling, you just practically need to wait and then collect your earnings later.

Stocks are great for passive income. However, you need to choose wisely when buying stocks. Don't buy on impulse, on a friend's suggestion (without any knowledge about stocks), or let your loyalty to a certain product or company cloud your judgment. You are looking for something that can bring you a lot of advantages and not display your devotion to a certain product. If the company that manufactures your favorite product has a good stock market standing, then buy some stocks if they offer it.

Savings

Saving money means setting aside a fixed or variable amount of money on a regular basis (every pay day) or whenever you have excess cash on hand. You may keep it in a bank, your home vault, piggy bank, or other places that you think your stash of cash would be safe. You can also use your money to buy stocks and turn it into savings.

When you invest, you use the money to buy an asset that you think is safe to acquire and can bring you acceptable rate of return. Some of the most productive investments are real estate, bonds, and stocks. The good thing about buying stock is that you don't need a large sum of money to buy it. There are good stocks that you can buy without the need to spend so much.

As a general rule, you must have enough savings to cover for six months worth of:

- bills payment (utilities, loan, insurance, and others)
- personal expenses (clothing, health and hygiene, and others)
- food
- other possible expenses

Understand that saving is different from investing, but you can turn the money that you will earn from your stock investment into savings. The idea is not to touch the earnings that you will get from your stocks, just keep it safe until the day comes when you really need to use it.

Return on Investment

ROI or return on investment measures the amount of return on your chosen investment against the cost of investment. It can help the investor evaluate the investment's efficiency. The investor can also draft a chart to see the efficiency of his/her investments and compare them with one another. You can use this formula to get the ROI:

$$ROI = \frac{\text{Earnings from Investment - Investment Cost}}{\text{Investment Cost}}$$

The 'Earnings from Investment' in the above formula pertains to the acquired proceeds from the sale of investment. The 'Investment Cost' is the total price that the investor paid for a particular investment, such as stocks. The difference that you get will from the two given data is the benefit or return. When you divide that by 'Investment Cost', you will get the ROI that is expressed in percentage form.

Since ROI is expressed in percentage form, it would be easy for you to compare the returns of your other investments and see the ones that can give the highest yield. You may want to consider investing more on the ones that can give you better advantage. Of course, you also need to weigh other factors that may suddenly influence the trend of a particular stock.

Stocks can give you a good return on investment, but you need to choose the right stocks to purchase and when to buy or sell them so you can get the most profits. You should keep track of your transaction costs. Other investors end up picking the wrong ROI figure because they fail to monitor the transaction cost.

Take a look at this example:

Company A is currently selling stocks for $5 a share. You are certain that it is a good investment and you have decided to buy 20 shares. You now have an investment cost of $100. If you have decided to sell your shares for $150, then your ROI is 50%. When you follow the given formula for ROI, you will have this:

$$\text{ROI} = \frac{150 - 100}{100} = \frac{50}{100} = .5 \text{ or } 50\%$$

To check if you get it right, simply multiply your investment cost of $100 by 1.5 and you will get 150. (Add '1' before a decimal point when you need to check.)

You can use ROI as your investment profitability gauge. The formula is easy to use and interpret, and you can apply it to a wide range of investments. If a certain investment yields negative ROI, you may want to do something immediately with that investment to avoid losing money. If you find another stock investment opportunity that can give higher return, you may choose to sell the stock that does not give the output that you expect while you can still offer it at a good price and still gain decent amount of profit.

If you also want to know your gross return, profit from stock sale, net return on investment, and current yield, you can use free online calculators.

Retirement

When you're in your twenties, retirement is probably the last thing you can think of. However, it is undeniable that making early preparations for your retirement is an excellent financial move.

Based on the past records, stocks have given the shareholders long-term gains that are larger than what other asset class can give. The large stocks have been generating an average of 10% return per year since 1926. The great thing about it is that at any time during the period of 20 years and above, stock investments remained stable. It makes investing in stocks a worthwhile endeavor and ideal for long-time savings as compared to stashing cash in you secret compartment.

You need to properly balance everything. If you spend all your time focusing on finding ways to save more money and providing value, you won't have a chance to enjoy the fruits of your labor to the fullest. On the other hand, if you don't save enough money or failed to provide value, you won't get to do much with your time.

Chapter 6: Before You Begin - Find Out the Type of Investor You Are

There is no doubt that stock investing provides a great opportunity to earn money. However, an investor must be able to know when is the best time to buy or sell stocks. Before you begin investing in stocks, you may want to know first what type of investor you are.

The Conservative Investor

A conservative investor is someone who does not take capital growth as utmost priority when investing. Instead, he seeks for stable investments that have the ability to flourish gradually and practically not susceptible to high volatility. A conservative investor usually obtains moderate capital growth and steady income stream. They may not get much from their investments, but they makes sure to get a steady flow of earnings regularly. The conservative investor is someone who is cautious in making investment decisions.

Fundamental Trader

A fundamental trader is someone who focuses on company-specific affairs to help them determine the right stock to buy and the best time to buy it. To depict this in another way, supposed this type of trader has decided to visit a shopping mall. A fundamental trader is someone who makes decisions based on fundamental things. They will visit each store, study the products that each store offers, and then make a decision whether to make a purchase or not. The same thing happens when it comes to buying stocks. They may study them first before he decides to make a purchase.

Trading on fundamentals can be a short-term or long-term endeavor. It is often associated more with the investing strategy known as buy and hold than short-term trading. Some trading strategies rely on split-second decisions and others depend on factors or trends that play out within the day. The fundamentals may remain the same for months or years.

The quarterly release of the target company's financial statement can provide valuable information regarding the firm's financial health or position in stock market. Changes or lack of it can give a trader a sort of signal whether to trade or not. A press release that brings bad news has the power to overturn everything in an instant.

Many investors find fundamental trading appealing because it is basically based on facts and logic – it practically ensures no room for errors. However, finding and deciphering the facts may take time and it is a research-intensive task.

Sentiment Trader

A sentiment trader does not try to outsmart the market by seeking securities that may bring huge earnings. Instead, he identifies the securities that move with the market's momentum.

Most sentiment traders combine the features of technical and fundamental analysis to help them identify and take part in the market movements. There are sentiment traders that aim to seize momentous movements in price and try to keep away from idle times. There are also traders that try to take advantage of indicators of excessive negative or positive sentiment that may provide sign of possible reversal in sentiment.

The key challenges that sentiment traders usually face are:

- Market volatility

- Trading costs

- Difficulty in making accurate predictions regarding market sentiment

If you think you are a conservative investor, your success depends on your ability to decipher the stocks that can give steady flow of income. You may not get large amounts of money, but you will always gain something with little to no risk involved.

The Intermediate Investor

The intermediate investor is someone who takes some risk but still makes certain that the initial capital that he invested will remain secure. This type of investor usually owns a rather volatile portfolio. These investors expects good (or near exceptional) capital growth. They may face some market fluctuations, which is unlikely to happen under normal market conditions. They usually own a balanced portfolio with assets that include a combination of bonds and stocks from established companies with good record. This trader may choose to make a small investment on riskier assets that can provide better capital growth.

Market Timer

A market timer is a trader who tries to guess whether a security will move up or down, and if such move can generate profit. To guess the direction of the movement, this trader checks the economic data or technical indicators. There are investors who strongly believe that the direction of market movement is impossible to predict.

Market timers with long-term track record won't be able to deny that it is quite challenging to achieve success using such method. Most investors know that they need to dedicate more time to gain reliable level of success. These investors believe that long-term strategies are lucrative and therefore more rewarding.

Arbitrage Trader

This trader usually buys and sells assets simultaneously in an attempt to gain substantial amount of profit from price differences of financial instruments that are related or identical.

Arbitrage traders buy a particular security in one market and sell it simultaneously at a higher price in another market, taking advantage of the price difference. It is considered a riskless trade that can provide sure profit to the investor.

Let us use foreign exchange in our example to illustrate. A trader buys a stock from a foreign exchange that is yet to adjust the price for the fluctuating exchange rate. The price of the foreign exchange at that time is undervalued when you compare it against the local exchange. The trader can take advantage of it and generate profit from the price disparity.

Arbitrage exists due to market inefficiencies. It provides a means to keep prices from deviating too much from fair value for a long time. Understand that it is impossible for all markets to impose uniform prices at the same time. A particular security may be traded at a lower price in one exchange market and higher price in another market.

An arbitrage trader may still gain a lot of profit now, but one should not underestimate the technology advancement. Soon, it may become difficult to gain profit from price disparity.

The intermediate investors may look like conservative investors at times, but they are not afraid to take some risks from time to time. If you are someone who wants to keep a balanced portfolio or is not willing to take risks all the time, then you are an intermediate investor. You may need to take extra amount of care when trading with risky stocks. You may gain more advantage than a conservative investor when you do that.

The Risk Taker

The risk takers are dynamic investors that are willing to trade with greater risk in an attempt to maximize profits. The investment portfolio of such trader could include stocks of young or new companies and emerging market equities. It may also contain higher percentage of stock than bonds.

Noise Trader

In noise trading, whenever a trader buys or sells something he does not refer to the fundamental data specific to a particular company that issues the securities. Noise traders commonly engage in short-term trades in an attempt to gain profit from different economic trends.

Noise traders over-react to any good or bad news surrounding the stock market and they also have poor timing. The technical analysis of statistics that the market activity has generated could turn into useless data because they won't be able to benefit from it. They can't properly look into the volume and past prices of the market that can somehow help them gain some insights on market activity and direction in the future.

Let us go back to the example that we had about the shopping mall. As compared to a fundamental analyst, a technical analyst may only sit outside and collects data regarding the number of people that each store may have. He does not care about the products being sold in each store. It is enough that he could see the number of people that each store can attract and help him arrive at a certain decision.

In reality, most people can be considered as noise traders. Only a number of individuals use fundamental analysis when making a decision regarding the investment.

If you are someone who's willing to trade stocks without knowing or weighing possible consequences that such trade may yield, you are a risk taker. You may be able to earn much profit at one time, and then lose some at other times if you are too reckless.

So, what type of investor are you? You may need to improve something to make sure that you will gain more profits. Knowing the characteristics or psyche of a good investor can help you a lot.

Nature of a Successful Investor

What do successful investors possess that brought them the things in life that they enjoy today? Read on and follow their lead.

Having Patience

Patience is a virtue – always remember that. It is important and prudent to have patience when investing in stocks for the long-term. You need to wait for the right time to buy or sell stocks, and don't get impatient.

Ability to Withstand Investment Loss

Even a conservative investor must be prepared and able to withstand the loss of sizeable portion of his stock market investment. There are certain uncontrollable factors that may lead to losses no matter how careful you are when you have decided to invest. The ability to withstand loss is an important component in investing. You need to be able to get your focus back after a huge blow so you can recover your losses. You suffered some losses, analyze the error (in case it is due to something that you did), learn from your mistakes, and get back on track.

Detecting Opportunities

A good investor must be able to detect good investment opportunity and grab it immediately. There are investors that are lucky enough to be born with a flair for sensing good investment opportunity. But, you can learn to be one. As you try to learn, always remember to exercise patience.

Seeing things with Contrarian Eyes

Many successful investors follow a contrarian investment style in which a trader goes against the prevailing market sentiment or trend. The trader typically buys assets that don't currently do well (but have potential to be good investments in the future) and then sell them when they become good.

Buying Low

In the tank is slang for poor performance. A sector, security, or market is said to be in the tank when its performance is way below expectations. When the market tanks, stock prices are usually low and it is good to buy shares of known good businesses that have appealing returns, make real profit, stock holder-friendly management, and some franchise value. Even if the stock price declines by at least 75%, the said companies will be able to come up with means to recover quickly.

Psychology of Investing in Stock Market

There are many skills and characteristics that a trader must be possess in order to gain success in financial markets. It is important to understand the fundamentals of a company as well as its inner workings. It is likewise significant to determine the trend direction. However, the most important is to have the capability to maintain discipline and suppress emotions.

Presence of Mind

It is common for traders to buy or sell stocks on short notice, and will likely need to make a decision in haste. To do such thing properly, they need to possess presence of mind so nothing can cloud their judgment. It is important to remember not to let emotions interfere in your investment decisions.

Deciphering Fear

When the trader's screen shows something horrendous to a stock holder and bad news about a certain stock fills the entire room, it is impossible for a trader not to get scared. The first thing that usually comes to mind is to liquidate or stop trading. If a trader does that, he may avoid losses but he would also miss his chance of making profits.

Fear is a natural occurrence when such thing happens, especially when it is something that can be perceived as threat. But, a trader must be clear about what he fears. A trader may be able to deal with fear better when he quantifies it or understands what he or she is afraid of.

It is important for a trader to isolate his or her fear during trading so he or she can remain focused.

Greed is Your most Horrible Foe

Greed is something that every investor should avoid. It can make the trader face the risk of getting whipsawed or lose his rationality. Greed is not easy to conquer because within each individual there's a desire to always do better than the others. A trader must be able to detect the presence of greed and should do everything in his power to come up with trade plans based on intelligent and rational judgment.

Giving Importance to Trading Rules

A trader or investor can set up his trading rules that can help him establish his limits and be able to exit a trade regardless of his emotions. A trader can set his price targets and when a target for a particular trade is met, it would be easy for him to make his exit.

He can also establish a rule that when a large trader graces the market, he may set it as a signal that it's time to get out. A trader can set other trading rules that can help him get out while he has the winning advantage or before his emotions affect him.

Designing a Trading Plan

When trading, it is important that a trader has substantial knowledge regarding the stocks that perked his interest. It is best to attend seminars, conferences, and conventions that can give information about the particular stock that you would like to trade. You also need to devote time doing some research. You can study the charts, read the trade journals, or do background work (such as industry analysis). You can use all the information that you gathered to design a trading plan that can turn you into a better trader.

Chapter 7: Open a Brokerage Account Now

Before you can start trading you need to open a brokerage account first. What is a brokerage account? It is an arrangement between a licensed brokerage firm and an investor. The investor deposits fund to the brokerage firm, which takes care of their client's investment orders. The investor is the sole owner of the assets in his brokerage account.

Opening a Brokerage Account

It is simple to open a brokerage account. There are different brokerage firms to choose from, and you decide which one to choose.

When you fill out the form, you will need to provide the following standard information:

- Name

- Address

- Date of birth (must be 18 years old and above)

- Contact number

- Driver's license or ID card issued by the state

- Type of account

- IRS tax ID number

- Signature of account holder

You also need to disclose the following to your broker-dealer:

- Investment objectives

- Employment status and other relevant information

- Net worth

- Annual income

Other Important Matters when Opening an Account

There are jurisdictions that allow confidential, coded accounts to be opened. The financial institution in which the account resides is compelled to protect the name of the investor.

The investor must submit a written acknowledgement that he owns the account and provide all the information that the broker-dealer needs to obtain. The broker-dealer checks to ensure that the statements and confirmations are printed with the account owner's alias instead of his real name. There are plenty of countries that permit secrecy in banking and Swiss bank accounts are well known for such practice. Even NYSE allows coded accounts.

The account holder must deposit the minimum amount that the brokerage firm requires. He or she can also transfer funds, which may take a few days to process. Once the account holder has completed the task, he can start investing.

Some Notes Regarding the Brokerage Firms

As a new investor, you will likely prefer to open a brokerage account with an online broker, which allows the investor to trade via its trading platform or website. Some of the best brokers also furnish their clients with analysis tools, significant research, and educational support to get things started.

Before opening an account, you may want to consider the following factors in choosing your broker:

1. Consider the **commission** that a particular broker may require you to give.

Almost all online brokers may charge between $5 and $10 per trade, although there are firms that offer commission-free trades. A broker usually gets his commission from traded stocks and exchange-traded funds. You may also need to pay a transaction fee for purchasing mutual funds.

2. Know the **account fees** that you need to pay.

The account fees usually include the inactivity fees, annual fees, and other charges for research and data as well as trading platforms. You can avoid paying these fees by choosing the right trader. However, you may not get quality services from a broker that doesn't charge such fees.

3. You need to determine the **frequency** of trade that you wish to make.

If you have decided to trade frequently, you may want to find a good broker that gets low commissions. Make sure to get a good broker or everything will just go down the drain. If you don't wish to trade often, choose a good broker that does not charge fees for inactivity.

4. Determine the **support** that you want to be provided for you.

You need to be clear on the kind of trading technology, customer support, and resources that you expect to get.

5. Know the minimum deposit that your chosen brokerage firm requires.

Not all brokerage firms have the same minimum deposit requirement. You may want to check their other requirements as well before you open an account.

Some Brokerage Firms

1. **Etrade**

Etrade is one of the discount brokerage firms that offer lower costs than full-service brokerage firms. Its web-based interface presents easy-to-use solutions and various resources for stock-plan participants, investors, and traders. Casual or infrequent investors may not find Etrade as the best platform because it comes with tiered fee pricing. Traders will surely appreciate its cutting-edge digital platforms with powerful tools and layout that is easy to navigate. However, don't expect a discount brokerage to offer all the things that a full-service brokerage can provide.

2. **Fidelity Investments**

Fidelity Investments offers a mobile platform and client website that novice and casual investors will find appealing. Even moderately active traders wills surely find it suitable when they place, research, and manage their trades. The client website can support conditional orders. The mobile app and client website have well-designed profile page that includes company profiles, financial, social sentiment, news, customizable chart, equity summary scores, and others.

Active and advanced traders can use and take advantage of Fidelity's customizable platform for desktop called Active Trader Pro, which can be accessed using Mac and PC. The platform allows the user to do market data streaming and advanced trading (that includes conditional orders and multi-trade ticket, which gives the trader the ability to put a maximum of 20 orders at once). It also provides portfolio management tools as well as access to alerts and orders to assist in distinguishing entry and exit strategies, news, charts, and positions.

3. Scottrade

Scottrade online brokerage firm offers online trading services, research tools, and a full line of investment products. The company provides self-directed traders and investors the capacity to invest on their own after they do their market research. All throughout the United States, Scottrade has more than 500 branch offices. Scottrade offers the following investment products:

4. TD Ameritrade

The well-designed web-based trading platform of TD Ameritrade provides the self-directed investors an easy access to the resources and tools that they need to research and handle their own trades. The investment products that traders can trade via TD Ameritrade include stocks, CDs, options, IPOs, ETFs, mutual funds, and bonds. It also supports future trading and forex.

To know more about the abovementioned brokerage firms, simply search them online.

Chapter 8: How to Properly Research A Company's Stock Prior to Investing

It is important to do a proper research first regarding the company stock that you would like to purchase. It is foolish to simply dive in and purchase some stocks without doing proper investigation prior to investing. For all you know, you may never have a chance to recover everything that you have lost.

Here are some of the places where you can get reliable information regarding your target company:

1. Investor Relations section of the Company's Website

2. Morning Star's website

3. Yahoo Finance

4. Google Finance

5. SEDAR (System for Electronic Document Analysis and Retrieval)

6. Securities Exchange Commission website

The First Step: Industry Research

1. Gather basic information regarding the industry where your target company belongs.

It is important to figure out the specific industry that your target company is in so you can check if that particular industry is doing well or not. You need to assess the size of the industry. Find out that particular industry's annual revenue as well as the number of companies under it. You also need to find out its annual revenue growth and the number of companies that join it per year.

2. Find out the names of the companies that have the largest market shares in a particular industry.

You also need to know the competitors of your target company and find out which one is doing better. It could give you a clear picture whether to proceed with your plan, wait for a bit, or totally drop the idea of buying a stock of your chosen company.

3. Try to find out the regulatory issues.

You need to look for government decisions, regulatory rulings, trade agreements, or barriers that might affect the industry at any given time. The regulatory rulings may be favorable or unfavorable for a particular industry. You need to make sure that your chosen company does not belong to the industry that might be facing or about to face unfavorable circumstances. You can visit the websites like Bloomberg, Wall Street Journal, or similar site to look for regulatory news.

4. Assess the industry's future trends.

You can predict the industry's future trends by analyzing its growth, movement, and plans for the coming years. Watch out for the consolidation or expansion in the number companies under that particular industry.

The Next Step: Understanding the Company

1. Learn everything regarding the company from the inside and outside.

It is important to know exactly how the company operates, its main products and/or services, the nature of its business, and how they generate profit. Let us assume that a lot of people praise a certain drink that made you decide to make an investment to the firm that produces it. It is prudent to know first the different types of drink that it makes, the target consumers, and other products that the company manufactures.

It is advisable to visit the business website's Investor Relations page to begin your research about the company. See if it contains company snapshot or corporate profile document, which can give you an idea about the business. On the same page, you need to look for its section for Investor Presentations.

A lot of companies that are publicly-traded furnish a PowerPoint presentation for investors every quarter. The presentation gives a business overview. It also depicts possible challenges, new developments, and results.

It is recommended to have a balanced view regarding the presented information that the documents contain. The presentation tends to show more of its positive side since the company has prepared it.

2. Read the comments of the experts on the business.

It pays to read the opinion of the experts when buying stock of a particular company. You can visit Morning Star's website and read what the experts and analysts have to say. The views of the experts can help you understand the rewards and risks of buying a particular stock.

However, you also need to be careful and make sure that you fully grasp the reasons behind any recommendation from the experts. Some analysts have ulterior motives for suggesting or recommending something.

You may also want to visit Yahoo Finance and Google Finance and benefit from their plethora of articles that highlight the latest news on stocks.

3. Educate yourself regarding the business' macroeconomic outlook.

There are major economic factors that could affect the business' performance and you need to be aware of them. Let us assume that you plan to buy a stock, particularly coal, at the most appropriate time because it proved to be a good investment. However, the economy of the huge purchaser of coal in the world suddenly declines and it could take years before it can see any improvement.

Such event indicates a depressing future for the prices of coal and may not be a good investment after all. Thankfully, you read expert analysis and news regarding the business you are interested in investing and saved yourself from possible trouble.

Aside from reading news and analysis, you also need to read company reports and see if there are issues that are currently affecting the stock that you plan to buy and may persist to influence the performance of the business.

4. Find out the competitive advantage of the company.

See if your target company earns more than its opponents due to its competitive advantages. Some of the competitive advantages that a company may have over the others are: similar quality products at a low price, unique items, better network distribution, and good customer service.

5. Know if the company maintains good management.

A well-managed company should not find much trouble in maintaining its good status. If a company is constantly dealing with internal management issues, it should give you a clear warning that investing in such company is not a wise decision to make.

6. Weigh everything and decide whether it is good to invest in such company.

After knowing all the things that you need to know regarding the company and finding out that there are some good and bad things surrounding the company, think carefully and weigh the good things against the bad. If you think you are taking too much risk in investing to such company, it is best to look elsewhere.

You also need to do a fundamental analysis and technical analysis on the stock that you want to purchase – that would be your last step before you decide whether to buy a certain stock or not. The next chapter will tell you more about them.

Chapter 9: How to Analyze Your Stock Before You Buy It

It is important for you to analyze your stock carefully before your buy it. Don't rely on the things that you hear and it is best to trust the information that you gathered yourself. It is advisable to learn how to conduct a fundamental analysis of the stock as well as technical analysis.

Performing Fundamental Analysis

Fundamental analysis entails examining a company's financial statements or information to determine the business' fair value as well as gain insight regarding its future performance.

Fundamental analysis does not deal with company's recent movements in price, stock chart, or the performance of stock price over a particular period of time. Its main focus is the business itself. Fundamental analysis wants to find out whether the company's revenue grows, can compete well with its competitors, how much profit it makes, and how much debt it owes.

The main concerns of the analysis are the three past and present financial documents: cash flow statement, income statement, and balance statement.

1. Study the company's revenues.

Studying the company's revenues over the past few years can give you an idea regarding where the business stands. Did it grow, decline, or remain stagnant?

You can use Morningstar.com to find the company's revenues. When you visit the site, type in your target stock, find your way to "Financials" and then click on "Income Statement". When you look at the top, you will find the company's revenues from 10 years back.

Ideally, you need to look for stable revenues that are bound to grow. Fluctuating revenues can tell you that the company is in a highly competitive industry.

2. Check the company's gross profit margin or GPM.

To get the profit margin, you need to get the gross profit first. You can get the gross profit by using this formula:

Gross Profit = Company's Earnings − (Raw Costs + Labor)

After doing that, you can calculate the gross profit margin using this formula:

$$\text{GPM} = \frac{\text{Gross Profit}}{\text{Total Revenues}}$$

Gross profit margin is expressed in percentage form.

For example, the company has revenue of $500,000, and $250,000 as its gross profits. When you divide 250,000 by 500,000 you will get .5 or 50%, which is the GPM for this particular case.

Visit Morningstar.com to check out stable gross profit and high GPMs. Remember this:

- A company with GPM over 40% all throughout is deemed strong.

- A business with 10% or less gross profit margin means that the company may be in an industry that is highly competitive and does not have any power to establish high prices.

Note that the various industries have different margins. You need to compare margins of competing companies to get valuable information.

4. Analyze the company's debt.

A company with large amount of debt is something that you need to consider carefully. The company chooses to pay high interest rates because it is unwilling or lacks the capability to finance its growth using its available funds.

Understand that there are companies that choose to borrow large amounts of money to sustain their operations and still attain growth. They would rather borrow money than rely on investors. They use leverage and increase both potential risk and profits.

You can use debt to equity ratio to determine the amount of debt a company owes. You need to divide the debt of company by the shareholders' equity. The result helps compare which party (debt or shareholders) owns the larger part of the business. A low ratio of debt to equity is a good sign.

5. Evaluate ROE or return on equity.

ROE determines the kind of profits that a company generates with the stock holders' investment. You can obtain the ROE when you divide company's profit by equity of shareholders. Morningstar.com also provides information regarding ROE. You can find the equity on the Balance Sheet.

ROE above 10% is already considered strong, but you still need to compare your target company's ROE with its competitors to make sure that you won't encounter unnecessary trouble.

6. Study the company's earnings growth.

An investor should be aware that whatever level of earnings growth a company may achieve, it would be the same with share price growth. That's why it is important to look at the past and future growth of the company. Take note that when we say earnings, we also mean profits.

When you visit Morningstar.com, you can look up "Net Income" or "Earnings per Share" to see past earnings growth over time. See if the earnings are steadily growing over time or declining.

You can use Yahoo Finance to find the estimates on future growth of a company.

7. Find out the company's P/E ratio or price-to-earnings ratio.

This ratio can help you find out the amount that you pay for every dollar of profits. Divide the price per share by per share earnings to get the ratio.

The stock can be seen as expensive if you pay more for a dollar of your chosen company's profits as compared to that of its competitors.

For example, your chosen company's price per share is $200 with $20 for every share as earnings. You will obtain a ratio of 10. It means a $10 payment is made for a dollar of your chosen company's earnings.

If the competitors of your chosen company obtain only a ratio of 5, your target company is deemed expensive.

8. Make a comparison table.

Once you have fully analyzed the stock and calculated the P/E ratio, you need to prepare a comparison table between your target company and its peers. To be blunt, you need to look for a company or companies that outshine their peers based on the mentioned factors above. You still need to look for a company with a lower P/E ratio than its competitors.

For example, company A and Company B both have gross profits of 40%, a return on equity of 9%, and steady growth for the past 12 years. However, Company A has a P/E of 14 while Company B has a P/E of 17. It is wise to invest with Company A because you can get better business without costing so much.

You can go to Morningstar.com to search for a list of a company's competitors.

Performing Technical Analysis

Technical analysis may seem complicated, but it is really all about supply and demand (remember our example where we used the shopping mall) to predict the direction of price trend. Technical analysis tries to comprehend the market sentiment behind the trends in price rather than studying the fundamental attributes of a stock.

1. Try to study Dow's theories behind technical analysis.

There are actually three Dow's theories that can guide the technical analyst with his approach to financial markets. The theories are as follows:

a. Market fluctuations exhibit all known information. Technical analysts can draw out the information they need from the price changes of a certain security and how well it fares in the market.

b. Price movements can be calculated and charted. Technical analysts acknowledge the fact that there are times when prices move arbitrarily. There are also times when it is easy to foresee the price trend. When that happens, you can easily buy low or sell high.

c. History can happen all over again.

It is quite difficult for a number of people to change their motivations in just one night. Traders are expected to give the same reaction to a particular situation that already happened in the past. A wise technical analyst should always remember the reaction of traders in the past so he can earn a lot of benefits in the present or future.

2. Look for speedy outcome.

Unlike fundamental analysis that depends on balance sheets and other data based on past few years, technical analysis focuses on data based on short periods of time that are usually no more than a month. Sometimes, it only needs a few minutes to assess everything.

3. Make it a habit to read charts, which can help you recognize price trends.

Graphs and charts of security prices are great tools for technical analysts to spot the general direction that the prices are headed. There are different trend classifications according to duration and type, and a technical analyst studies them all to make intelligent predictions.

4. Learn the concepts of support and resistance.

Support refers to the lowest price that a security has reached before more demands pour in and cause the price to go up. Resistance refers to the highest price that a security has reached before a large number of stock owners trade their shares and cause the price to go down.

When you look at a chart illustrating channel lines, the line at the bottom of the chart represents support (the security's floor price). The line at the top represents resistance (ceiling price). Resistance and support levels are used to verify the presence of a trend as well as to detect any trend reversal. It is advisable not to buy when stocks are trading near support level.

5. Take notice of the volume of trades.

If there's a substantial increase in volume of trading even as the price increases significantly, the trend may be valid. If there's only a slight increase in trading volume or even falls as the price increases, the trend may be due to a reverse.

6. Take advantage of moving averages.

A moving average is a sequence of computed averages quantified over successive, measured time intervals. Moving averages filter out the misleading highs and lows to present clear overall trends.

Technical analysis is commonly used for short-term trading, while fundamental analysis is most ideal for someone who wants to become a long-term stock holder of a company.

Chapter 10: The Top 15 Metrics You Must Examine Before Buying Any Stock

There are numerous metrics that can help you in your decision making when it's finally time for you to purchase a stock.

1. **Revenue**

Take note that revenue comes before profits. The other term for revenue is sales. It is the amount of money that a buyers exchange for products or services. Increasing revenue means that the demand for the products or services of a particular company is also rising. When revenue is declining, it means that the demand for the products or services is also falling.

2. **Expenses**

On the opposite side of revenue are expenses, which are expected to occur in order to create worthy products or services. Expenses are all the expenditures of a business to operate smoothly. Expenses include research and development, raw materials, interest, taxes, payroll, and others. To get the exact amount of profit, you need to deduct expenses from revenue.

3. **Price to Earnings Ratio** (P/E)

The **P/E ratio** can give you a clear view regarding the amount that you need to pay for every dollar of profits.

Basically, a high P/E ratio implies that shareholders are looking forward to a future with higher earnings from their shares. A low P/E ratio signifies that the company is doing remarkably well as compared to its past trends or the company may be undervalued as of the moment.

4. Debt to Equity Ratio

The debt to equity ratio can be computed as total liabilities (or debt) divided by equity. The ratio can help determine the company's leverage to its owned value. A company must aim for a low debt to equity ratio. A high ratio means that the company must continuously meet the obligation to pay the debtor to avoid insolvency.

5. Dividend Yield Ratio

To obtain the dividend yield ratio, take the dividend per share and divide it by its share price.

As the price of stock falls, the dividend yield increases and vice versa. A conservative investor would rather invest in large cap stocks with high dividend yield.

A young investor who is willing to take calculated risk to acquire high gain from his investment may not appreciate high dividend yield stocks. The reason being is that it won't provide huge capital appreciation. However, it is recommended to keep some stocks with high yield dividend in your portfolio.

6. Price to Book Ratio

This ratio compares the cost of stock to its book value, which is the equity balance of a company's balance sheet divided by the number of outstanding shares. Businesses that rely on equity or assets to generate cash flows will surely appreciate the data that the ratio yields. It does not bring any benefit to franchises and businesses with negative equity.

7. PEG Ratio

You can use this formula to calculate PEG ratio:

$$PEG = \frac{\text{Price to Earnings Ratio}}{\text{Growth Rate x 100}}$$

This ratio takes growth rate into account when valuation is being considered. A company that enjoys an annual growth rate of 12% should have a higher P/E ratio than its competitor with only 4% growth rate. It is said that it is a bargain if a PEG ratio is below one.

8. Current Ratio

The current ratio shows the company's liquidity if it has enough to pay its debt. Higher current ratio can be viewed as better than low current ratio. However, a figure that's too high may be a sign of the company's inefficiency in using their financial resources.

9. Return on Equity (ROE)

ROE shows the annual percentage of profit that a company generates on its equity. It can be obtained when you take the net income and divide it by equity. ROE can provide useful gauge in assessing the speed of a company's growth.

10. Return on Asset (ROA)

Assets are important in scaling profits. ROA is one of the most effective profitability ratios to determine the financial capability of a company. It is also one of the simplest profitability ratios. You only need to get the net income and divide it by total assets.

11. **Operating Profit Margin**

To get the operating margin, divide operating profit by revenue. Operating profit includes the majority of expenses, except taxes or interest. Operating profit margin presents the business' profitability without shrouding earnings power with taxes or interest.

12. **Free Cash Flow** (FCF)

A number of investors prefer free cash flow over earnings because they believe that cash does not lie. The cash that a business is able to generate after using the money to expand or maintain its asset base is represented by FCF. Use this formula to get FCF:

Free Cash Flow = Operating Cash Flow – Capital Expenditures

FCF is important because it makes it possible for a company to grab opportunities that may boost shareholder value.

13. **Return on Invested Capital** (ROIC)

ROIC recognizes the profit that the company makes on the money that its capital base retains. ROIC is always expressed in percentage form and typically presented as an annualized value. To determine if the business is creating value, ROIC is compared to the capital cost of the company.

14. **Industry Price Earning**

The industry P/E ratio is similar to company P/E ratio. Both offer the same benefits. Here is the formula for industry P/E ratio:

$$\text{Industry P/E Ratio} = \frac{\text{Total P/E Ratio of All Companies (within the same industry)}}{\text{Total Number of Companies within the Same Industry}}$$

15. Management

A company with solid management, together with the workers, is bound to succeed. A management that is capable of making strategic decisions is every company's blessing. You can regard it as a captain of the ship that stirs the company to the right direction. The management of publicly traded company takes care of generating value for stock holders. If a company does not have good management, don't expect to get the earnings that you wish to get.

Chapter 11: Determine Your Basic Investment Philosophy and Goals

You need a reason when you are about to do a meager task and you need a plan when you intend to do something big. But, if you are planning to deal with a life-changing task, you need to establish your own philosophy.

Establishing your Goals and Philosophy

Before you start investing, you need to establish your investment philosophy and goals. The investment philosophy is a collection of ideas and goals that can guide you when you have decided to start investing. It can guide you in your decision making and help you carry out your plans. You need to be clear regarding the reasons that made you want to invest in stocks.

Know Your Goal

When you create your investment philosophy, you need to be clear about what you wish to get from your investments. Do you plan to use the earnings from your investment for your retirement? Are you thinking of taking a vacation with the entire family once you have enough earnings from your investment? Once you have established your goal, it would be easy to determine the time that you need to invest and how much money must be invested.

When you are clear with your goals, you can determine the best course action to follow and attain success.

Find the Level of Risk You're Willing to Take

Even a conservative investor must be prepared for some risk. It is important to be clear on the level of risk that you are comfortable with. Understand that you need to take risk sometimes in order to grow. Otherwise, kiss your goals goodbye.

There will always be highs and lows when you start investing in stocks, but there are things that you can do to avoid possible losses (or keep them minimal). Understand that you can still gain the losses that you may have and probably earn some extras later on.

Beginners in stock investing need to take some risk to make their portfolio grow at a fitting rate. Remember that you should not take more risks than you can handle because once the stocks begin to plummet, all you might do is freak out. You may lose your focus and possible earnings at the same time.

You can ask a financial advisor to guide you during your early years of stock trading. You can be on your own when you feel like you are strong enough to trade on your own.

Keep Your Goals and Philosophy Simple

As a beginner in the world of stock investing, you need to keep everything simple. Don't try to chase the latest hot stock because you might get burned. A simple investment plan does not mean you will only make meager earnings. Keep in mind that you are still trying to grasp everything and it is best to take it a step at a time.

If you have simple philosophy and goals, it would be easy for you to comply and achieve them with less trouble. You will become more confident when you have finally achieved one of your goals.

Understand that this book is not about risky day trading, speculation, or get-rich-quick scheme. This book aims to help novice investors to start investing in blue chip companies that have already proven their worth through time. These companies hold long history and dominance in the stock market.

You will find real value and appreciation if you choose to have a long-term investment of more than ten years. You will be able to have a sound investment that can help you generate:

1. Dividend passive income

2. Investment for your retirement

3. Build capital through re-investment of dividends

Dividend Passive Income

Earning dividend on dividend-paying stocks is one of the easiest ways to earn passive income. The more the company earns, the larger the dividend. It is the primary reason why you should choose a good company or corporation to invest your money – the more profits they earn, so do you.

Understand that the dividend that you receive may vary, unless you are a preferred stock holder or owns shares that earn a specific amount of dividend. If you want to make sure that you will get a steady flow of dividends, you may choose to invest only in blue chip companies.

You can reinvest the earned dividend to buy additional shares, which will earn additional dividend later.

Invest for Retirement

How much money you need to invest for retirement depends on a number of things? You might want to consider when to start investing, the type of stock to invest in, the number of shares that you want to buy, companies to buy from, and when to retire.

Typically, the retirement age is 60. There are people who prefer to retire when they are in their 40's or 50's. There are also some people who want to retire at age 30. It is important to think clearly about the age that you want to retire so you can plan your retirement well. Take note that you don't need to reach 60 years old to retire, you can retire at a much younger age.

Conventional wisdom dictates that your retirement portfolio should be 40% bonds and 60% stocks. The said allocations must slowly and steadily shift more to bonds as you get older. The reason for this is because your investment time horizon becomes short as you age.

The Journal of Financial Planning has published a 2014 study, which claimed that the ideal stock allocation for early retirement should be 30%. It further stated that it should slowly shift more away from stocks as a person ages. The shift is known as rising equity glide path. The study based its recommendation on the idea that retirees should limit their stock exposure early in retirement to avoid experiencing possible poor returns during the first few years. They need to increase their stock assets later on to earn more.

Build Capital through Reinvestment of Dividends

If you want a steady, more dependable income from your investments, you need to invest in companies that pay dividends regularly. Dividend paying stocks attract more investors, especially now that we have low-interest rate environment.

Once your stocks start earning dividends, you can build capital if you reinvest your dividends. You can purchase another stock using the dividends that you earned. Your new stock will earn a dividend soon and if you have enough earnings to buy another stock, you can reinvest it.

You can decide when you must reinvest your dividends (check your goals), and there's no rule that says you cannot keep reinvesting your dividends. You don't even need to buy stock in the same company. You can explore other possibilities. If you have enough data to prove that reinvesting in the same company is more profitable, then you can reinvest in the same company.

However, I would highly recommend that you take advantage of **Dividend Reinvestment Plan or DRIP**, which is an automated strategy where the dividends are given in form of additional shares in the company.

Chapter 12: How to Use Dividend and Dividend Reinvestment Plan to Compound Your Stock Investing Even More

Many investors, beginners, and veterans, find dividend-paying stocks appealing. The said stocks offer lower risk investment, a great opportunity to generate earnings for a long time, and suitable for retirement or ideal source of income for retirees.

If you are keen on gaining extra earnings from dividends, it is necessary to invest only in dividend-paying companies with solid track record under their name. Take a look at some of their benefits:

- Worry-free investing

- Steady flow of earnings

- Opportunity to grow your investment

- Lower risk

It is also important to think carefully about the companies that you want to invest in and the ones that you want to stay away from. If you have a financial advisor, you can discuss things and create a plan. Make sure to stay true to your goals and investment philosophy.

It is important to know the safety, sustainability, and predictability of the dividend that your chosen company offers. You can determine a particular company's performance by getting reliable information regarding the company. Chapter 8 has a list of different sources of information if you need to know more about a certain company.

The Supremacy of Compounding

Compounding happens when the generated earnings are reinvested to generate more earnings. Dividend compounding happens when you use the dividends you earned to buy more shares that can give you greater dividends.

To illustrate, let us assume that you need to make a choice: take the $1,000 right now or take one dollar that would double in value each day for 15 days. Which do you think is a better choice? Look at the table below to see the earnings of a dollar in each passing day:

Day	Value
1	$1
2	$2
3	$4
4	$8
5	$16
6	$32
7	$64
8	$128
9	$256
10	$512
11	$1,024
12	$2,048
13	$4,096
14	$8,192
15	$16,384

Compounding dividends works in the same manner – you are doubling your earnings when you keep reinvesting your dividends. Understand that the figures in the given table are exaggerated (but might also come true with the right investment).

Dividend Reinvestment Plan (DRIP)

Shareholders can reinvest variable amounts in a company through DRIP, which is also a long-term investment scheme. Shareholders can buy shares or fraction of shares (if the dividend earned is less than the cost of one stock) at a time. The cost per share could be as little as $10.

Instead of issuing dividend check to investors, the body that runs the DRIP (could be the company, brokerage firm, or transfer agent) will use the money to buy additional shares under the investor's name.

Getting Started

Not all companies offer DRIP and you need to search which ones offer the reinvestment plan. Aside from companies, there are also brokerage firms that offer DRIP. If you can't find a company that offers DRIP, you can always go to a brokerage firm.

If your target company has DRIP, you need to know who runs the plan – your chosen company or a transfer agent. You are required to buy shares in your chosen company so you can set up an account.

It is best to register your name on the stock certificate. Know that not all companies have specific characteristics of DRIP. There are companies that allow shareholders to purchase only using their dividends, while others allow additional cash purchase aside from the reinvestment.

You can also enroll via a traditional broker, but you need to make sure that the broker buys in your name and not using the "street name" or the name of the broker. You cannot participate unless the shares are under your name. Remember that you need to pay the broker his commission.

Broker-operated or synthetic DRIPs are easier to set up than doing it yourself. All you need is contact your broker. The only drawback is that you cannot buy a fraction of share in case your dividend is not enough to buy a whole share. If your dividend is $30 and the stock that you want to invest in via a brokerage firm costs $20, the remaining $10 will be in cash instead of a fraction of share (this is only possible with company offered DRIPs or true DRIPs). A true DRIP lets you enjoy the full benefits of compounding.

There also share purchase plans or SPPs that allow you to acquire additional shares and you don't need to pay brokerage commissions. This is suitable for investors who want to make regular contributions.

The great thing about synthetic DRIP is that you only need to exert minimal effort because the broker practically does all the work for you. The broker takes care of reinvestment and other things so you can do so much more with your time.

Later on, you will be able to learn other methods where you can get so much more from your investments.

Taxation

Many people thought that DRIPs are not subject to tax because the stock holder is actually not receiving any dividend at all. You need to understand that DRIPs are still subject to tax because a dividend has been paid and it is still considered an income, although reinvested.

Like any stock, capital gains from DRIP shares will only be calculated when the stock gets sold.

Chapter 13: How to Buy Your First Stock to Start Your Stock Market Investment Journey

You already know that it is prudent to invest in blue chip companies because they provide secure, steady earnings. However, you still need to choose the company that you are comfortable dealing with.

From the previous chapters, you already know the things to look for and you have a list of sources of information that can help you evaluate a certain company. The next thing you need to do is buy a stock.

Here are the things that you need to do with your first stock:

1. **You need to set a budget for buying the stock.**

You only need to start small (as little as $100.00) as you are still trying to familiarize yourself. Remember that greed breeds evil and you need to stick with your investment philosophy and goals.

2. Determine how many shares you would like purchase.

Buy stocks according to your budget, and don't add more money so you can buy as many stocks as you want.

3. Don't forget to set aside a brokerage commission cost.

Your broker relies on commission in exchange for the services that he will render.

4. Place your order through your online brokerage account.

Once you opened a brokerage account and everything has been settled, you can begin placing your order through your account.

5. It usually takes 3 business days for the order to be completed.

You already know the different types of orders and you also need to understand that sometimes it takes a while to complete the order.

6. Monitor your stock after a week to know how it fares and get a sense of your purchase.

Although you have a broker that does the trading for you, you still need to monitor your stock so you can come up with a good investment plan.

7. Always take time to monitor the news, development, and other things about the company so always know what's going on.

Sometimes, there are unforeseen events that may affect the standing of the company you invest in. You can act immediately if you are fully aware about the things that go on with the company.

8. **Check your dividend payment in 3 months time and every quarter thereafter.**

Is your dividend being reinvested in purchasing more shares? You may need to make some adjustments and you can ask your financial adviser about it.

9. **Turn your attention in finding another great company to invest in.**

You only need to repeat everything that you did when you buy your first stock.

Chapter 14: How to Build a Portfolio of Stocks to Invest in

Your portfolio must be able to sustain your future capital needs and give you peace of mind. As an investor, you can design a portfolio according to your goals and strategies. Here are some of the things that can help you build your stocks portfolio:

1. **Determine the asset allocation that you think is suitable for you.**

It is important to ascertain your investment goals and financial situation first before you decide to create a portfolio. You need to consider the following:

- your age

- amount of investment capital

- the length of time you want your investment to grow

- future capital needs

- your investment philosophy

A young man or woman who's just starting his or her career requires a different investment strategy as compared to a 50-year-old mother looking for ways to live in comfort when she retires and help her child graduate from college.

You need to be honest about the risk tolerance that you can take. Ask yourself if you can risk some money for a chance to gain higher returns even though everything is uncertain. It is foolish to even try it when you know that it would only bring stress that can affect your health.

Depending on your investment goals, you need to determine what kind of portfolio you want to create based on the following:

a. **Conservative Portfolio**

If you choose this type of portfolio, you need to allocate 75% of your capital on stocks and 25% on bonds.

b. **Aggressive Portfolio**

Choosing this type of portfolio means you are investing 100% of your capital on stocks.

c. **Balanced Portfolio**

This type of portfolio requires the investor to put 50% of his capital on stocks and 50% on bonds.

d. **Safe**

If you have decided to choose this type of portfolio, it means you are willing to invest 100% of your capital on bonds.

2. **Create your portfolio according to your design.**

When you are certain about the asset allocation that you want, you can now proceed with dividing your capital according to the set allocations of your chosen profile.

The different asset classes can be split into subclasses, which offer different potential returns and risks. You can divide your allocation for stock between different market caps and sectors as well as foreign and domestic stocks. You can also divide your allocation for bond.

There are different ways to choose the securities and assets to satisfy your strategy for asset allocation. Always analyze the potential and quality of the investment you intend to have. Remember that not all stocks and bonds are the same:

a. **Choosing Stock**

In your portfolio's equity portion, you need to consider the stock type, sector, and market cap when picking stocks that can satisfy the risk level that you are willing to carry. Study the companies using stock screeners to shortlist prospective picks to know possible risks and opportunities. You must monitor the price changes regularly and make sure that you know the latest news on the company.

b. **Choosing Bond**

Include these factors when choosing bonds: bond type, maturity, rating, and general interest rate.

c. **Mutual Funds**

The money managers are responsible for investing the capital of the mutual funds to obtain capital gains and profit for the investors of the fund. These funds cover a wide array of asset classes. You can hold bonds and stocks that the money or fund managers have carefully researched and picked. The fund managers usually deduct their service fees from your returns. Index funds, on the other hand, tend to have lower fees since they only emulate an established index and they can be managed passively.

d. **Exchange-Traded Funds** (ETFs)

ETFs are like mutual funds, in essence. You can trade them in the same way as you deal with stocks. ETFs are passively managed and offer cost savings as compared to mutual funds and, at the same time, they provide diversification. ETFs also cover a wide selection of asset classes. They can provide a lot of help to your portfolio.

3. **Rebalance your portfolio**.

There's a need to periodically analyze and rebalance your portfolio because your initial weightings may get affected by the market movements. You must quantitatively classify the investments and verify the proportion of their worth to the whole when you need to assess the actual asset allocation of your portfolio.

Things like risk tolerance, future needs, and financial situation may likely change over time. In case these things change, you may need to make necessary adjustments to your portfolio.

4. **You need to rebalance strategically**.

Once you have determined which overweighted securities must be cut, you need to decide which underweighted securities must be purchased with the proceeds you obtained from selling the other securities. You can refer to step 2 when choosing your securities.

You also need to consider the tax implications of portfolio readjustment when you sell assets to rebalance your portfolio.

It is imperative that you maintain your diversification above anything else throughout the entire process of portfolio creation – always keep that in mind. Owning securities from each class of assets should not be your only goal. You need to diversify within each class. See to it that your holdings within a certain asset class are distributed across a range of industry sectors and subclasses.

Chapter 15: Be Aware of the Costs to Investing in Stocks

When you invest in stocks, there are other costs or fees that you need to pay and consider. You need to consider the broker's commission (please refer to Chapter 7 for details), tax implications, and opportunity costs.

Tax Implications

Aside from investment income, the federal government also taxes dividends, capital gains, real estate, and more. If you earn from a transaction, it is best to expect that you need to pay a certain tax.

Tax on Dividends

The dividend that you receive may be taxed at the rates that apply to long-term capital gain income or ordinary rates for income. If you are a shareholder of a qualified foreign corporation or a domestic corporation, your dividends will be taxed according to the rates that long-term capital gains need to pay. The dividends that most companies pay are after-tax profits, and it means that the taxman has taken a cut already. The shareholders need not worry about the 15% preferential tax rate on qualified dividends if the company's headquarters is in the USA. The same goes with companies outside of the country but has a double-taxation agreement with USA.

Non-qualified dividends, which are paid by foreign entities or companies, must pay a regular income tax that is usually higher.

Tax on Capital Gains

Tax on capital gains depends on the length of time that the investor has the security in his possession. If it's a long-term investment (one year and above), the tax rate is 15%. However, taxpayers with high income must pay 20%. Taxpayers that are considered high-rate should also pay the healthcare surtax. All in all, they need to pay 23.8%.

Short-term investment (less than one year) must pay a regular income tax rates.

Taxation and Bonds

An investor does not need to pay capital gain if he or she buys a bond at par value and hold on to it until it matures. However, the investor must pay the tax rate of either long-term or short-term capital gain when he sells the bond before it matures and he obtains profit from the sale – the same with stock.

Corporate bonds' interest payments are subject to state and federal taxes. Federal bonds' interest payments are subject to federal taxes but free from state tax.

Wash Sales and Tax Losses

As an investor, you may offset capital gains against capital losses acquired in the same taxable year or from the previous years. Each year, an individual may deduct net capital losses of $3,000 maximum against other taxable income.

When you harvest tax losses, you can reduce your capital gains tax liability. If your portfolio has one or more stocks that drop below your cost basis, you can sell and achieve a capital loss for tax purposes.

However, there is a catch. The IRS regards the sale and repurchase of a largely similar security within a month as a wash sale, which disallows entry of capital loss in the present tax year.

Opportunity Cost

Opportunity cost is a benefit that an individual could have obtained, but let it slipped through his fingers in favor of another course of action. It represents a renounced alternative when a certain decision is made. In investing, it is the return difference between the investment that you decided to pass up and the one that you have chosen.

The different measures that can help you determine the profitability of certain investments were already discussed. When you are already in stock market investing for quite some time, there may be some investments that you thought to be profitable but opted to choose the other one instead. It is also important to consider each option's opportunity cost that could help you make a wise decision when there's a need to rebalance your portfolio. The formula you need to use is this one:

Opportunity Cost = Return of the First Option - Return of Selected Option

No matter which option you picked, the potential profit that you missed by not investing in that particular option is known as the opportunity cost.

For now, it is enough to know the basics. You will know more as you become more familiar with stock investing.

Chapter 16: When to Sell a Stock

The ideal scenario is that you should invest in a company forever. But, we have to admit that it is realistically impossible to happen (unless, maybe, the company is the king of kings in the realm of blue chip companies). There are certain factors and circumstances that may lead to a company's financial demise – corruption and other unforeseen events, economic sabotage, political unrest, inner conflicts, and etc.

As a wise investor, you need to know the right time to sell your stocks. When it is evident that there's no more hope for the company to recover, you need to sell to avoid incurring losses and preserve your capital.

However, you can also decide to sell if you can see that it is the best time to let go of your stocks to gain much profit. You can choose to invest the money in a more profitable company.

You may also choose to sell if you need additional fund for a certain business venture that you want to pursue (not necessarily investing in other securities).

When It Hits Your Target Price

Most investors set a target price at which they would be willing to sell their stocks. When you initially buy your stocks, it is important that each stock purchase comes with an analysis on the stock's worth, and other pertinent data that can help you determine the target price when you need to sell it.

Selling your stock when the price has doubled is a good move. However, it is quite challenging (even for a veteran stock investor) to set a single price target. It is best to have a price range as your target and it is more realistic.

There's a Drop in the Fundamentals

You already know the importance of fundamental analysis in stock investing and how to do it. You need to periodically monitor the fundamentals of your stocks to make sure that they continue to yield expected output. If you notice a decline in the fundamentals, it is best to perform a thorough analysis and decide to sell when you can clearly see that there's something wrong with the company.

There's a Better Opportunity

Before purchasing or replacing your current stock, always compare the potential gains between the current stock and the new target stock. If the new or alternative stock is way better than your current one, it is best to sell the current stock and purchase the better one.

These are just some of the things that may push you to sell your stocks. The financial tools listed in Chapter 8 can help a lot when making important decision regarding your investment.

Chapter 17: How to Monitor and Grow Your Stocks

You can grow your stocks by rebalancing your portfolio when there's a need to do so. Remember the factors that you need to consider. There's also a need to monitor your stocks to make sure that you will consistently gain or only suffer minor losses. Understand that there are things that may suddenly affect the market trend that may not necessarily require you to sell your stocks right away.

You Need to Monitor the Business rather than the Price of Stock

There are times when the price of a particular stock keeps fluctuating. At first glance, it is quite alarming. As a wise investor, you need to monitor the business of the company where you bought some stocks. Understand also that sometimes some unknown situation may occur that can temporarily affects the stock price. Focus on the performance of the business and not the stock price. As long as the business is doing great, you can expect to get your future earnings from the company.

You need to monitor the quarterly reports of the company as well as the progress of business. You already have a list of financial tools that you can use and all you need to do is spare some time to research the data that you need to find.

You may also decide to rebalance your portfolio if you think that doing so can bring you a lot of benefits and advantages.

Analyze the Numbers

Your knowledge in technical analysis can also help you analyze the numbers or figures in the reports. You will be able to know whether the sale is growing or not. If it's not growing, what is the reason behind it? Has the company increased its debt or issued more shares? There's always a reason behind each number.

You may need to study the financial statements of the company where you bought your stocks. Look if the different ratios give favorable results or there's a need to be alarmed and re-visit your investment portfolio once more.

Performance of Management

There are times when a change in management could affect the overall performance of the business. You need to know the management's sentiment towards the shareholders. Does the management pay dividends on time? What is the current focus of the management? You need to consider these and other related things to decide whether you will still get benefits and gains from your investment given the current performance of the management.

Chapter 18: Recommendations for Further Learning in Investing in Stocks

This is just the beginning of your journey in stock investing. You can continue to improve to learn more that can help you with your stock market investing endeavor.

Here are some of the helpful sources of information that I recommend that you can use to deepen your knowledge.

Books:

1. Intelligent Investor by Benjamin Graham (must read book if you want to investing in value companies and investment school of though)

2. The Essays of Warrant Buffet by Warren Buffet and Lawrence Cunningham

3. Common Stocks and Uncommon Profits by Philip Fisher

4. How to Make Money in Stock by William J. O'Neil

Websites:

- Investopedia.com

- Berkshire Hathaway's annual Chairman's (Warren Buffet's) letters (these are gold mines of wisdoms that are shared from Buffet with his investors (shareholders) since its inception.

- Morning Star.com

- Financial section of any major newspaper (if you are serious about stock market investing, then you will need to regularly read this section)

Conclusion

Thank you again for buying this book on investing in the stock market!

I hope this book was able to help you learn everything that a beginner in stock market investing should know to start investing the right way and intelligently.

Stock market investing is an easily accessible way to grow your money without a lot money to begin with. You can start investing in stocks with as little as $100 dollars. Follow the steps that I shared with you in this guide and you will be pleasantly surprised with your results and at the same build the confidence to manage your own finances and start building your wealth one stock at a time.

The next step is to put everything that you learned in this book into practice and don't forget to learn more about stock investing to polish your investment skills further.

Finally, if you enjoyed this book, then I'd like to ask you for a favor, would you be kind enough to leave a review for this book on Amazon? It'd be greatly appreciated!

Thank you and best of luck!

Regards,

Alex M. Peter

www.ingramcontent.com/pod-product-compliance
Lightning Source LLC
Chambersburg PA
CBHW070303230526
45470CB00002B/706